A GUIDE TO **ALGOL** PROGRAMMING

McCracken D.D.

A Guide to FORTRAN Programming
A Guide to IBM 1401 Programming
A Guide to ALGOL Programming
A Guide to COBOL Programming
Digital Computer Programming

McCracken D.D., Weiss H. and Lee T.H.

Programming Business Computers

McCracken D.D. and Dorn W.S.

Numerical Methods and Fortran Programming

DANIEL D. McCRACKEN

McCRACKEN ASSOCIATES, INC.

a guide to
ALGOL
programming

JOHN WILEY & SONS, INC., New York · London · Sydney

Library of Congress Catalog Card Number: 62-17464

Printed in the United States of America

ISBN 471-0-58234-4

PREFACE

This book is written for the person who wants to get a rapid grasp of the use of a computer in the solution of problems in science and engineering. The application of a computer to such problems is greatly simplified by the use of ALGOL, or a similar language, because it is not necessary to learn the details of computer operation.

The book does considerably more, however, than explain ALGOL.

* It develops for the newcomer to computing the fundamental idea of an algorithm. That is, since computers do not accept *problem* statements, how does one go about transforming a problem statement into a problem-solving *procedure*, stated in a language acceptable to a computer? (This also applies, of course, even when a computer is not involved.) Experience shows that it is here that students have the most difficulty in getting started with computer work.

* It includes many examples and case studies that show how computers are applied in science and engineering. This material is drawn from a wide variety of application areas and is used as the means for a further elaboration of how to write an algorithm.

* It includes illustrations of some of the basic ideas and techniques of numerical analysis. It will therefore tie in nicely with a combined course in computer programming and numerical analysis.

* Nearly 20 per cent of the book is devoted to exercises and the answers to about half of them. It is therefore quite suitable both for self-study and for use in formal courses with homework. Experience indicates that a serious student can do *all* the exercises in 30 to 40 hours; anyone who does so—or even does half of them—will have acquired a firm grasp of the subject.

* It is organized so that each reader can easily select the material he needs. The person who wants only a quick view of programming can study Chapters 1 to 3; Chapters 4 and 5 develop all the remaining material needed for the majority of applications; Chapters 6 and 7 bring in the rest of the ALGOL language features; Chapter 8 suggests input and output methods for the person who has no actual system to study. The person who already knows programming and is interested only in a quick explanation of ALGOL can skip Chapters 1 and 8 and skim the examples and exercises; he will have no difficulty at all in picking out the third of the text that is specifically about ALGOL.

* It brings in, at various relevant points, a number of matters of computer efficiency. In few cases, however, are they peculiar to ALGOL, so that the reader can get a good idea of how to make effective use of a computer.

In addition to the obvious usefulness of this book for self-study of ALGOL or of scientific computing in general, it is anticipated that it will find application in several types of formal courses.

1. It can be used as the text for a short seminar in engineering, science, or mathematics. A six-week session of two to three hours per week could cover the first five chapters and leave time for a good term problem.

2. It can be used as the text for a one-semester hour course, which provides more than enough time to cover the material. The

extra time can be used to give a survey of machine-language coding or to let the students run a number of practice problems and a sizable term problem.

3. It can be used as the text for a supplement to some other course. Covering the fundamentals of ALGOL will take only a few hours away from the course, and this "lost" time can be recovered by the assignment of more realistic problems in the primary subject matter. A particularly happy combination is numerical analysis and ALGOL, by which the time spent in teaching ALGOL will be more than recovered.

4. Students in an industrial course in ALGOL programming will find the book useful as an elaboration of the presentation in the reference manual and as a guide to the ways in which ALGOL can be applied in the solution of realistic problems.

It is a pleasure to acknowledge the many and varied contributions of the following people: Fred Gruenberger of the RAND Corporation; Bill Youden and Joe Wegstein of the National Bureau of Standards; Rollin Thompson and Brad MacKenzie of Burroughs; George Forsythe and John Herriot of Stanford University; Dick Lesser of Cornell University; Bernie Galler of the University of Michigan; Don Knuth of Cal Tech; Mike Woodger of the National Physical Laboratory, Teddington, England; Bill Lee of IBM; Bob Bemer of Remington Rand; Robert Hux of RCA; John Borst, a student at New York University; and Steve Borst, a student at the Johns Hopkins University. To the many others who helped in some way, unfortunately too numerous to mention, my sincere appreciation. Mrs. Bea R. Boxer did most of the typing.

DANIEL D. McCRACKEN

Ossining, New York
June 1962

CONTENTS

INTRODUCTION: HOW TO USE THIS
BOOK EFFECTIVELY

To obtain the most value from a study of this book, the reader should be aware of a few matters concerning its content and organization.

1. The word ALGOL refers to a language for stating computational procedures, independent of any computer, and also to a computer program called a "processor" that is able to translate a procedure stated in ALGOL into the elementary "instructions" that a computer is capable of executing. Thus ALGOL is useful for communication between humans and for communication to a machine. The treatment in this book is applicable to both purposes.

To be able to use ALGOL for communicating computational procedures to a computer, there must be an ALGOL processor available for it. Because of the variety of the problems that arise in constructing these processors, not all computer systems for which there is an ALGOL processor are able to accept the full generality of the language discussed in this book. Furthermore, there are minor variations from one ALGOL processor to the next, even in things that are included in all of them; these are mostly detailed matters of how certain symbols are written.

The presentation in this book covers the full ALGOL language, with one or two exceptions. The reader who is concerned with a particular processor, therefore, will need to find out exactly what his system includes and how it operates. For this purpose, it will ordinarily be necessary to have access to a reference manual for the particular system. This book does not replace the reference manual, and vice versa; the two complement each other.

2. Fully half of the book is devoted to examples and exercises, including nine case studies. These studies are intended to illustrate the ALGOL language features and to show how computers can be used for scientific computation. They go even further by attempting to show how one can approach the formulation of a procedure to solve a given problem. This is perhaps the most important thing the beginner in computing has to learn. Many of the exercises are designed specifically to provide practice in this matter. There are answers to about half of the exercises, so that the student may check his understanding of the concepts involved. Some of the exercises at the ends of the chapters are considerably more difficult than the earlier ones; in some cases they will suggest term problems.

3. The speed and depth of learning will be enhanced by actual practice in preparing and running problems—early and often. It is, of course, not *necessary* to have a computer at hand in order to master the subject, but if one is available it should be utilized at every opportunity.

1. COMPUTERS, ALGORITHMS, AND ALGOL

1.1 Typical Applications of Computers

Electronic computers are widely used to assist in solving the problems of science, engineering, and business. This use is based on their ability to operate at great speed, to produce accurate results, to store large quantities of information, and to carry out long and complex sequences of operations without human intervention.

Computer applications generally fall into one of the following categories, although it should be noted at the outset that the dividing line between them is rather indefinite in some cases.

Commercial applications. Many computers are employed in the processing of business data. How much did each man in a factory earn last week? What accounts of a department store are delinquent? How much of each inventory item is on hand and how much on order? How much of each product was sold in the preceding month and how do sales compare with those of the same period last year? Such problems are generally characterized by a large volume of data, with relatively little computation on each item. Despite the simplicity of the calculations usually involved, such work is nevertheless challenging because of the amount of data and the measures that must be taken to achieve speed of processing and accuracy of the results.

Engineering. Computers are heavily used in many branches of engineering. The design of a new airplane requires thousands of hours of computer time to investigate the interrelated requirements of structures, aerodynamics, powerplant, and control system as they would operate under numerous flight conditions. The design of a chemical plant involves calculations of capacities, operating conditions, and yields under a variety of circumstances. The design of an electric transmission line requires study of the loads that would be imposed on the different sections of the line as the consumption changed and as unusual conditions arose.

It may be noted in this sampling that the computer does not "solve the problem." Instead, it helps to explore the alternatives. We do not ask the computer, "How should I build this new device?" but rather, "How would the device work under this set of conditions if I built it this way?" There are many ways in which the equipment could be built; there are various operating conditions to consider, and there are several different and even conflicting goals to be balanced. The computer *cannot* enumerate the design choices, specify the operating conditions, decide what the goals are, or determine the trade-offs among conflicting goals. It *can*, usually, provide us with great assistance in predicting the consequences of *our* choices in these matters.

Research. This category covers a lot of ground, some of which is not too far from engineering. Representative examples would be problems in the theory of numbers, study of molecular and nuclear structure, research into numerical methods of solving mathematical problems, and the study of methods for describing economic processes.

Process control. Many physical and business situations change so rapidly and require such quick response that a human being would find it difficult or impossible to keep up. An extreme example is the prediction of the orbit of a satellite from radar data received shortly after launching. No human being could possibly carry out the calculations to decide whether the trajectory would be satisfactory within the time available. Many other applications of a less dramatic nature could be cited.

Non-numerical applications. This is another category that, to a certain extent, overlaps with others. Examples would include translation of languages by computer, the simulation of one computer by another, attempts to simulate intelligent behavior, and the "translation" from the language of ALGOL (or some similar system) to the language of a particular computer. It will be realized that some of these are also research, but others are used routinely.

1.2   The Steps in "Solving a Problem" with a Computer

We have already seen that there is much more to "solving a problem" with a computer than the work the computer does. It may be instructive to outline the complete process of setting up a typical engineering problem for computer solution to see just what the human does and what the computer does.

Problem identification and goal definition. This is the question of choosing a general approach, deciding what combination of goals the system must satisfy, and specifying the conditions under which it will be required to operate. In some applications this is very simple; in others it may take months.

Mathematical description. There are, as a rule, several ways to describe a process mathematically; one of these must be chosen, or a new one must be developed if no standard method is applicable.

This is the area of applied mathematics, mathematical physics, operations research, and the like.

Numerical analysis. The mathematical formulation of the problem may not be directly translatable to the language of the computer, since the computer can only do arithmetic and make simple quantitative decisions. Trigonometric functions, differential equations, integrals, square roots, and logarithms, to name a few common examples, must be expressed in terms of arithmetic operations. Furthermore, it must be established that any errors inherent in the data or introduced by the computations do not invalidate the results.

Computer programming. The numerical procedure must be stated as a precisely defined set of computer operations. There are usually two steps to this part. In the first the sequence of operations is written in graphical form in a *block diagram,* as we shall see in Section 1.3. Then the procedure must be stated in a language that can be "understood" by the computer or which can be understood after a preliminary translation stage. ALGOL is such a language. This book is devoted almost entirely to the subject of programming.

Program checkout. There are so many chances to make mistakes in programming that most programs do not work when first tried. The errors must be located and the program thoroughly tested to be sure that it does perform as desired. The computer is used during this step.

Production. Now, finally, the program can be combined with data and run. In a typical situation many sets of data are run off at one time. This step may take a few seconds to many hours, depending on the problem and the computer.

Interpretation. As we have noted, the results printed by the computer do not always constitute a final "answer" to the "problem." The user of the computer must interpret the results to see what they mean in terms of the combination of goals that the proposed system must satisfy.* Frequently it will be necessary to repeat some or all of the preceding steps until the problem is really "solved."

Several conclusions may be drawn from this discussion. First, the computer does not solve

---

* If the combination of goals can be stated in numerical terms, it is sometimes possible for the computer to assist in the first part of this analysis.

problems, it only follows carefully defined computational procedures. Second, a computer does not relieve the user of the responsibility of planning the work carefully; in fact, the computer demands much more careful planning. The computer is faster and more accurate, but it cannot decide how to proceed or what to do with the results. Third, a computer does not in any way reduce the need for a full and detailed understanding of the problem area or for a thorough knowledge of the mathematics involved. Finally, it should be realized that the programming step—the primary subject of this book—is only one part of the complete process; it may not even take a majority of the time of the user.

This is not meant to minimize the importance of programming nor to suggest that it can be done haphazardly. Programming can be a sizable task and is frequently fascinating in its own right. We simply wish to suggest at the beginning that programming be viewed in the perspective of the full range of activities.

1.3 What Is an Algorithm?

Let us look now at the question of specifying a problem-solving procedure to a computer. In some ways it is similar to giving instructions to a person doing the calculations with pencil and paper, but in certain other important respects it is quite different. The following considerations must always be kept in mind when working with a computer.

1. Everything must be specified *in advance;* once you have written a procedure and entered it into the machine for execution *you are no longer in the picture.* The execution of the procedure is done entirely by the machine, with no intervention on your part. Naturally, if the results are not what you need, you get back into the picture and revise your procedure, but during the execution the machine is in complete control. This means that you must state beforehand exactly what should be done in every circumstance that can reasonably arise. If something special should be done when a certain variable becomes negative, you must write its handling into the procedure *in advance.* If you would like the machine to stop when a certain number gets too large so that you can investigate what is happening, you must so signify. If printed

results are required as soon as some measure of convergence is satisfied, you must define this criterion in precise terms.

2. A computer cannot exercise judgment unless it has been provided with explicit directions for making a decision. It must always be remembered that a computer has no common sense. If you enter angles in degrees into a computer system that has been set up to accept angles in radians, the computer will blindly carry out the computations specified even though the results are meaningless. Any person familiar with trigonometry would raise a questioning eyebrow if handed a sheet of data with angles of 300 radians—but not the computer. Hand a person a column of numbers to be added, and you don't have to tell him how many numbers there are or show him some other way to recognize the end of the list—but you do with a computer. It is simply not possible to say to a computer, "If anything unusual turns up, give me a call." Not unless you can *specify in advance* what constitutes "anything unusual."

These considerations are incorporated in the idea of an *algorithm,* which is a precise and complete statement of a computational procedure. This is the heart of learning how to use a computer effectively: how to go about devising an algorithm, what constitutes a good algorithm, and the way to write an algorithm in a language that is acceptable to a computer.

Let us consider what is meant by an algorithm in terms of a simple example.

Problem. Find x, given that $ax^2 + bx + c = 0$.

We should begin by emphasizing that computers cannot do much with *problems.* It would be possible to enter this equation into a computer in some suitably coded form, but doing so would not lead to a solution. We must give the computer a *procedure* for computing the solution. It happens that there are several ways to solve this problem in terms of numerical procedures, of which we must choose one. The most familiar is to use the formulas

$$x_1 = \frac{-b + \sqrt{b^2 - 4ac}}{2a}$$

and

$$x_2 = \frac{-b - \sqrt{b^2 - 4ac}}{2a}$$

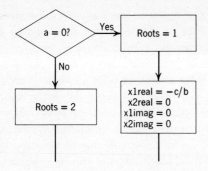

Figure 1.1. The first part of a block diagram of a method for finding the roots of a quadratic equation.

These formulas form the basis of an algorithm in that they suggest a procedure for solving the given problem. If we substitute numerical values for a, b, and c into these formulas, we will usually get values for x_1 and x_2, thus solving the problem. The formulas are not themselves a complete algorithm, however. We need three more things: a precise statement of what to do with exceptional cases, a precise statement of the sequence of operations, and a "language" for expressing the procedure.

One exceptional case suggests itself immediately. If a is zero, the formulas do not apply; we must go back to the original equation and note that in such a case the equation is linear, not quadratic, giving only one root. Now *we* must make a decision—one that the computer cannot possibly make for us: what do we *want* to do in such a situation? Is this a normal occurrence for which provision should be made? Does this indicate a data error? If we were to assume that a would never properly be zero, we could let such a coefficient signal the end of a deck of data cards. Is this to be done?

A computer problem usually requires many decisions such as this one. The computer can be set up to do whatever we want it to do, within limits, but it cannot decide which choice should be made.

Without trying to fabricate enough details of a hypothetical application to permit a realistic discussion of what would be best in this case, let us assume that a can be zero without indicating anything special. We will compute the one root, set the other "root" equal to zero, and print a 1 in a column set up to indicate the number of roots. When there are two roots, we will print a 2 in this column.

A second exception is of a different kind. The formulas as written apply whether the roots are real or complex, but the computational procedure is quite different in the two cases. In fact, if a computer procedure is set up on the assumption that all roots are real, complex roots will not be computed correctly at all. For the real case the output consists of two numbers; for the complex case the real and imaginary parts of the two roots make four numbers to be printed. If the computer is expected to handle complex roots correctly, space for the two additional numbers must be provided. Once again we have a decision: are complex roots a normal occurrence or do they signal data errors? (Some physical situations described by the equation should never lead to complex roots.)

In any case, the algorithm should include a test for a negative discriminant, $b^2 - 4ac$. Whatever is to be done about it, we must not try blindly to take the square root of a negative number, using a computational procedure designed for real numbers. Let us assume that complex roots are normal and set up the algorithm to distinguish between the real and complex cases.

Having decided what to do with the obvious special cases, we are ready to start working out the exact sequence of operations in a procedure that will solve the problem.

What should we do first? We had better start with a test to determine whether a is zero, because the formulas do not apply if it is. Figure 1.1 is a *block diagram* (also called a *flow chart*) of this test and the actions to be carried out if a is zero. (This is actually just the beginning of a complete block diagram of the algorithm; the lines leaving the boxes must go somewhere, to be decided on later.)

In the reasonably simple block diagramming notation used in this book a *diamond* denotes a test or comparison. The test is shown here in the form of a question to which the answer is yes or no. A *rectangle* denotes almost any kind of computer operation except a test or an input/output action. All rectangles in this example result in the assignment of a new value to one or more variables, which is generally what a rectangular box contains. In fact, this kind of operation is so common and so fundamental that we might call a rectangular box an *assignment* box.

We note in Figure 1.1 that after asking whether a is zero we set a variable named *Roots* equal to the number of roots in either case. Also shown is the assignment box that indicates the computations decided on for the case in which a is zero. Names for these quantities have been made up more or less arbitrarily; it is a good idea to make names suggestive of the quantities they represent, as we have done here.

The large assignment box embodies a completely arbitrary choice of another kind. If one root is to be set equal to zero and the other to $-c/b$, which shall we call $x1real$ and which $x2real$? In this example it makes absolutely no difference, and the choice was made by tossing a coin. In other problems there might be some reason for doing one or the other.

If we look ahead a bit, we will realize that the discriminant $b^2 - 4ac$ is going to turn up in a number of places. Why not give it a name and compute it once, rather than repeating the same arithmetic steps several times? Having done so, we can test the sign of the discriminant to determine whether the procedure should follow the real or the complex path. Figure 1.2 shows the incomplete block diagram as it now stands. It may be noted that a different notation has been used in the box that indicates the testing of the discriminant. A colon represents any kind of comparison, the nature of which is then shown on the arrows leading out of the decision box. The question-mark type and the colon type are both acceptable decision boxes.

This much of the block diagram embodies another decision on our part: if the discriminant is zero, we follow the path for the real case. Taking the square root of the zero discriminant and going through the separate computations of the two roots is an apparent waste of computer time. Why not make a test for a zero discriminant and simply set both roots equal to $-b/2a$ if it is zero? The course taken here is based on the assumption that a, b, and c are taken from physical measurements, in which case it is extremely unlikely that the discriminant would be *exactly* zero. Making a test for zero in every case would in fact waste more time than would be saved in the rare cases in which the discriminant was zero.

Now we are ready to compute the roots. Looking ahead again, we see that the square root of the discriminant will be needed in two places in the real case. Why not compute it once and use the result wherever needed? The block diagram of Figure 1.3 is based on this decision. The rest of the procedure for the real case is a simple statement of the formulas, with the imaginary parts set equal to zero.

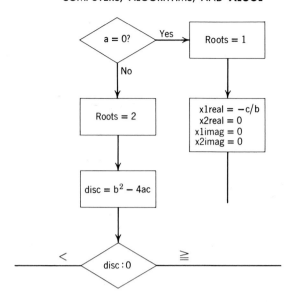

Figure 1.2. Continuation of the block diagram of Figure 1.1.

In the complex case there is no need to compute the square root of the discriminant in advance because the root will appear only once in the rest of the procedure. This is made possible by taking advantage of a characteristic of complex roots: they always occur in conjugate pairs; that is, the real parts are the same and the imaginary parts are the negative of each other. The block diagram shows clearly the sequence of computational steps in calculating the four numbers that comprise the answer in the complex case.

It must be realized that even though we are computing complex roots all the arithmetic in this procedure is real. It is necessary to set up the operations to handle the real and imaginary parts of a complex number separately, which is all any digital computer can do. Furthermore, in the case of the imaginary square roots of a negative number the procedure is set up to take the square root of the *negative* of the negative discriminant, since a procedure based on operations with real numbers cannot take the square root of a negative quantity.

One final question must be considered: what is the source of the coefficients a, b, and c and what is to be done with the results? If this algorithm is to be regarded simply as a general procedure for finding the roots of a quadratic equation, then we might assume that a previous procedure would have generated the coefficients and that some following procedure would make use of the results.

Let us assume here, however, that this is supposed to be a complete procedure for a computer, with the coefficients read from cards and the results to be printed. There is no need to delve into the details of computer input and output here; we can simply indicate the card reading and the printing and leave the details until later. Note the shape of an *input/output* box in Figure 1.4.

While we are completing the block diagram, we may as well make one more slight improvement. As the diagram has been developed so far, there are two places at which we set the imaginary parts of the roots equal to zero. No complications are introduced if we delete one of these (for the special real case in which *a* is zero) and draw an arrow down to the box that does the same thing for the general real case. The complete block diagram is shown in Figure 1.4.

The algorithm is now just about completed. All that remains is to express it in a language that is understandable to a computer. Figure 1.5 shows the procedure written in ALGOL, which is such a language. Since the remainder of the book is devoted to a detailed explanation of ALGOL and how to use it, there is no point in presenting a detailed explanation of this ALGOL algorithm. With a few pointers, however, it is nevertheless possible to read it rather easily.

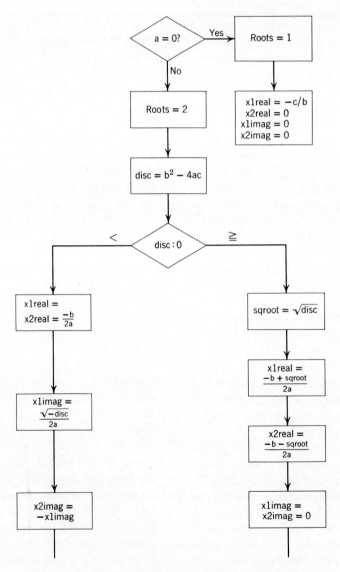

Figure 1.3. Continuation of the block diagram of Figure 1.2.

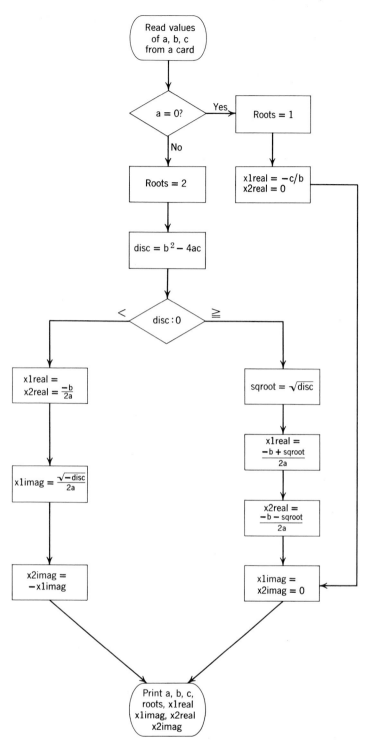

Figure 1.4. Block diagram of a method for finding the roots of a quadratic equation.

The Read and Print operations that call for the reading of data and the printing of the answers are not strictly part of ALGOL. Facilities for such operations are a part of any computer system that can accept an ALGOL procedure, but they do represent an extension of the basic language. Words printed in boldface have special meaning in ALGOL. Semicolons separate *statements,* which are commands to the computer to carry out actions. When several statements are grouped to form a *compound statement,* they are enclosed between the words **begin** and **end,** which are called *statement brackets.* The colon in front of some equal signs can be ignored for the present. The if-statement allows an operation to be done only if some condition is satisfied; if the condition is not met, the entire statement (which is compound here) following the **then** is skipped. The words *zeros* and *output* are *labels* with which it is possible to specify *transfers of control,* as is done in the seventh line. Spacing between characters and the placement of statements in lines carries no significance; all such matters of arrangement may be employed however one wishes, to improve readability.

This algorithm, slightly modified, was run on a computer with several sets of data. The results are shown in Figure 1.6, just as they were printed by the machine.

1.4 What Is ALGOL?

ALGOL, which stands for ALGOrithmic Language, is exactly what its name implies: a language for expressing algorithms. It was developed by an international group of computer people between 1957 and 1960. Improvements and modifications are still being suggested, but the language is more or less stabilized at the present time as that defined in the May 1960 issue of the *Communications* of the Association for Computing Machinery, in "Report on the Algorithmic Language ALGOL 60," edited by Peter Naur. The "60" distinguishes the present language from a preliminary one, sometimes referred to as ALGOL 58, and from later versions that may in time be sufficiently different to warrant a new designation.

ALGOL is intended to serve two rather different purposes. One is the communication of algorithms among people; computational procedures must be expressed precisely whether or not a computer is immediately involved. The other purpose is to describe procedures in a form that can be accepted by a computer, causing it to carry out the desired processing.

The second should be amplified somewhat. A procedure written in ALGOL cannot be executed *directly* by present computers; the ALGOL pro-

```
Read (a, b, c);
if a = 0 then
        begin
        Roots : = 1;
        x1real : = −c/b;
        x2real : = 0;
        go to zeros
        end;
Roots : = 2;
disc : = b ↑ 2 − 4 × a × c;
if disc < 0 then
        begin
        x1real : = x2real : = −b/(2 × a);
        x1imag : = sqrt (−disc)/(2 × a);
        x2imag : = −x1imag;
        go to output
        end;
sqroot : = sqrt (disc);
x1real : = (−b + sqroot)/(2 × a);
x2real : = (−b − sqroot)/(2 × a);
zeros: x1imag : = x2imag : = 0;
output: Print (a, b, c, x1real, x1imag, x2real, x2imag, Roots);
```

Figure 1.5. An ALGOL program segment to find the roots of a quadratic equation.

gram must first be translated into *machine language*. Present computers can carry out only simple operations such as adding two numbers, storing a result, reading a card, or transferring to a different group of instructions if two numbers are not equal. The language of ALGOL, which is much more sophisticated, must be translated into the machine's own elementary language before the program can be executed. This translation, however, can be done by the machine itself, under control of a separate program of machine instructions called an ALGOL *processor*.

Let us review the steps in getting an ALGOL program executed on a computer. A *source program* is written in ALGOL; this is simply the algorithm to solve the problem, written as a set of ALGOL statements. This program, *not* including any data, is translated by an ALGOL processor into an *object program*, consisting of elementary machine instructions for the machine on which the problem is to be solved. The object program is not executed during this processing; no data is read; no results are printed or punched. Now, with the program expressed in terms the machine can "understand," it is executed: data is read, the compu-

tations carried out, and results written. The processor, which is itself a computer program, is not involved during this execution phase.

When ALGOL is used to express algorithms to a computer, it can be viewed as a *language together with a processor program,* and the word is used with both meanings.

Clearly, to use ALGOL as a computer source program language, an ALGOL processor must be available for the machine on which the object program is to be run. Furthermore, if all features of ALGOL are to be utilized, the ALGOL processor must be able to accept all features. In fact, ALGOL processors are not available for all computers, and some processors accept only a subset of ALGOL. Therefore, the reader who wishes to use ALGOL as a computer programming language must ascertain what processor is available to him and what its characteristics are.

The reader should also realize that almost no ALGOL processor accepts the exact notation used in the ALGOL 60 Report and in the bulk of this book. This *reference language* uses symbols and notational conventions that are not directly acceptable as input for most computers, such as the

A	B	C	X1REAL	X1IMAG	X2REAL	X2IMAG	ROOTS
1.000	-2.000	1.000	1.000	.000	1.000	.000	2
1.000	-7.000	10.000	5.000	.000	2.000	.000	2
6.000	-9.000	-6.000	2.000	.000	-.500	.000	2
1.000	.000	-1.000	1.000	.000	-1.000	.000	2
1.000	.000	1.000	.000	1.000	.000	-1.000	2
1.000	-2.000	2.000	1.000	1.000	1.000	-1.000	2
4.000	24.000	20.000	-1.000	.000	-5.000	.000	2
100.000	200.000	100.000	-1.000	.000	-1.000	.000	2
.000	63.900	-221.300	3.463	.000	.000	.000	1
1.000	-4.000	8.739	2.000	2.176	2.000	-2.176	2
4.129	-14.811	-61.002	6.035	.000	-2.448	.000	2
-1.016	.499	-49.573	.245	-6.980	.245	6.980	2
.000	568.981	-490.652	.862	.000	.000	.000	1

Figure 1.6

symbol $>$ for "greater than" and an arrow to denote exponentiation. Such matters are handled by some kind of transliteration, such as writing the letters "GR" for $>$ and ** to denote exponentiation. The language formed when all such transliterations have been established is called a *hardware representation*. Different computers, in general, have different hardware representations of ALGOL.

There is also an intermediate level called the *Publication Language*, which may be used to write algorithms for man-to-man communication. It permits considerable freedom in notational matters (Greek letters, for instance) that are not included in the reference language and that might not be acceptable in a particular hardware representation.

Most of this book is based on the reference language. It should therefore be useful whether or not the reader is interested in ALGOL as a computer source program language.

EXERCISES

The point of these exercises is to give you practice in defining a precise procedure to operate on variables about which you know only the general characteristics. You are asked in each case to develop an algorithm, expressed as a block diagram. You need not show input or output operations.

Answers to starred exercises are given at the back of the book.

*1. Place whichever of the variables X and Y is larger in BIG. If $X = Y$, place either of them in BIG.

2. Place whichever of the variables X, Y, and Z is largest in BIG. (This can be done with only two comparisons. Establish whether X or Y is larger, place it in BIG, then determine whether what is now in BIG is less than Z, and if so place Z in BIG.)

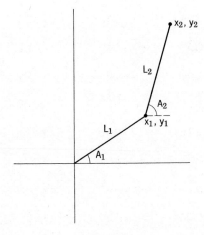

Figure 1.7

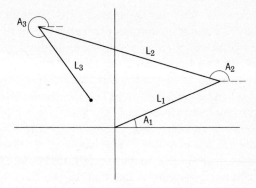

Figure 1.8

*3. $Y1$, $Y2$, and $Y3$ are the ordinates of three points on a curve. If $Y2$ is a *local maximum*, that is, if $Y1 < Y2$ and $Y2 > Y3$, place $Y2$ in *Top* and place a 1 in *Max*; otherwise, do nothing.

*4. If $0.999 < X < 1.001$, set *test* equal to 1; otherwise set *test* equal to zero.

*5. Given a directed line segment beginning at the origin, together with its length and the angle it makes with the x-axis, write expressions for x_1 and y_1, the coordinates of its endpoints.

6. Given two line segments as sketched in Figure 1.7, where you are given the length of each and the angle each makes with the x-axis. Find x_2 and y_2, the coordinates of the endpoint of the second segment. (You are given no information about orientation; you do not know which quadrant either angle is in or the relative sizes of the lengths and angles. This uncertainty will create no problems as long as you do not try to take advantage of any special characteristics of the sketch.)

*7. Given three line segments, as sketched in Figure 1.8, and the same type of information as in Exercise 6, compute the value of *closure*, the distance of the end of the last segment from the origin.

8. Given four line segments that supposedly form a square, as sketched in Figure 1.9. If the error of closure is less than 1% of the sum of the lengths of the four sides *and* no side equals zero, then set the variable *OK* equal to 1; otherwise set *OK* equal to zero.

9. The system

$$ax + by = c$$
$$dx + ey = f$$

has no solutions, one unique solution, or an infinite number of solutions. The criteria for the three cases can be stated as follows, where we have also given the actions you should perform.

a. If $ae - bd = 0$, but $af - cd \neq 0$ or $bf - ce \neq 0$, there are no solutions; set *solutions* equal to zero.

b. If $ae - bd \neq 0$, there is one unique solution; compute it (get the values of x and y) and set *solutions* equal to 1.

c. If $ae - bd = af - cd = bf - ce = 0$, there are an infinite number of solutions; set *solutions* equal to 2.

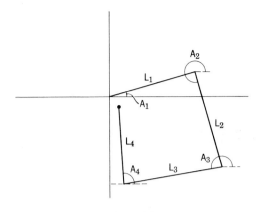

Figure 1.9

*10. Given the line $y = ax + b$ and the circle $x^2 + y^2 = r^2$, set *solutions* equal to 0, 1, or 2, depending on whether the line and the circle do not intersect, are tangent, or intersect at two points, respectively. (Solve the two equations simultaneously and use the discriminant of the resulting quadratic equation.)

*11. Given the following tax table, compute *tax* from *earnings*.

Annual Earnings	Tax
Less than $2000.00	Zero
$2000.00 or more but less than $5000.00	2% of the amount over $2000.00
$5000.00 or more	$60.00, plus 5% of the amount over $5000.00

*12. The present United States Social Security tax is $3\frac{1}{8}\%$ of earnings up to $4800 in one year. Given a man's previous year-to-date earnings ($PYTD$) and this week's *earnings*, compute his *tax* on this week's earnings and his new year-to-date ($NYTD$). You should take into account the following possibilities:

   a. The man has earned $4800 or more before this week, in which case the tax is zero.

   b. The man has not earned $4800, including this week's earnings, in which case the tax is $3\frac{1}{8}\%$ of this week's earnings.

   c. Before this week he has not earned $4800, but including this week he has, in which case his tax is $3\frac{1}{8}\%$ of the difference between $4800 and his previous year-to-date earnings.

13. The current United States Withholding Tax on a weekly salary can be computed as follows: 18% of the difference between a man's gross pay and $13 times the number of dependents he claims. Given *gross* and *dependents*, compute the *tax*. (Do not assume that there is always a tax: a man may not have earned more than the dependency allowance.)

14. Suppose that the squares in a tic-tac-toe game are numbered as shown in Figure 1.10 and that you are given $N1$, $N2$, and $N3$, the numbers of three squares. Assume that $N1 < N2 < N3$. If the three squares so designated are in a line, set *line* equal to 1; otherwise, set *line* equal to zero. Can you suggest a way of renumbering the squares that would greatly simplify the test?

*15. Given two times, both expressed in hours and minutes since midnight, such as 0145, 1130, or 2350. You are guaranteed that $h_1 m_1$, the first time, is earlier than $h_2 m_2$, the second time, and that they are less than 24 hours apart. Compute the difference between them in *minutes*.

16. A certain parlor game requires determining the number of common letters in two five-letter words, neither of which has any duplicated letters. For instance, there are no common letters in BLACK and WHITE, one common letter in BLACK and MAUVE, and five common letters in NAILS and SNAIL. Outline in words a method of doing this; a complete block diagram would require techniques not yet discussed.

17. The algorithm for finding the roots of a quadratic equation shown in Figure 1.4 gives correct results for every combination of zero coefficients except $a = b = 0$, but it takes no advantage of special conditions such as $b = 0$ or $c = 0$. Redraw the block diagram to make use of any special conditions. If any two coefficients or all three are zero, set both roots equal to zero (admitting that this does not make complete sense for the "equation" $c = 0$).

The result will be a block diagram with many more boxes than the one in Figure 1.4, but the new version will take fewer computational steps when the special cases arise. This situation exemplifies a common choice in programming: whether to write an algorithm that is big but fast or one that is compact but slow.

1	2	3
4	5	6
7	8	9

Figure 1.10

2. NUMBERS, VARIABLES, AND EXPRESSIONS

2.1 Numbers

We must now leave the fundamental concept of an algorithm long enough to learn the vocabulary of ALGOL. With the vocabulary in hand, he shall be able in succeeding chapters to develop illustrative algorithms as new language elements are introduced.

We begin by considering the two types of numbers that may be used in an ALGOL program: *integer* and *real*.

An integer is simply a positive or negative whole number, including zero. In the reference language there is no consideration of maximum permissible sizes of quantities; in any hardware representation there is some reasonable limit. Different hardware representations in general have different limits, but a typical figure would be ten decimal digits.

The following are acceptable integer numbers:

$$0$$
$$6$$
$$+400$$
$$-1234$$
$$70000000$$

The following are *not* acceptable integer numbers:

17.38 (decimal point not allowed)

14.0 (decimal point not allowed, even though a whole number is represented)

$2_{10}8$ (exponent part—see below—not allowed, even though a whole number is represented)

1,000,000 (commas not permitted)

123456789000 (probably too large for most hardware representations)

An integer must be a whole number; an ALGOL *real* number may be a whole number or have a fractional part. In a hardware representation the important difference between the integer and real types is that real quantities are stored in the computer in what is called *floating point* form. This is a method of representation similar to scientific notation, in which a number is treated as a fraction (between 0.1 and 1.0), times a power of 10. The quantity so represented must either be zero or lie between reasonable limits established for each computer system. A typical range is 10^{-50} to 10^{50}

The main point of the floating point system is that the programmer is relieved of any problems concerning the handling of decimal points. All questions of lining up decimal points before addition or subtraction and of determining the location of the decimal point after multiplication and division are automatically taken care of by the computer. This is the reason for the term "floating point."

Any number that appears in literal explicit form in an ALGOL program is called a *number*, whereas a quantity that is given an *identifier* (name) is called a *variable*. For instance, we shall see shortly that the following are *assignment statements:*

$$I := 2$$

$$X := A + 12.7$$

Here 2 and 12.7 are numbers; I, X, and A are variables.

An integer number may be written with or without a sign; it must not be written with a decimal point. A real number may be written in just about any of the familiar forms, except that its last character must not be a decimal point. It may be written with or without a sign and with or without a decimal point. It may be written as a number multiplied by an integral power of 10 by placing 10 below the line followed by a signed or unsigned integer.* The lowered 10 and the integer power are called the *exponent part.*

Most quantities in an ALGOL program are ordinarily of the real type, since in dealing with physical data it is necessary to work with nonintegral amounts. Integer quantities are in most cases used for special purposes required by the structure of ALGOL, as we shall see in later chapters.

The following are acceptable real numbers:

0.0	$-_{10}7$
6.0	00074
.873	$_{10}-4$
0.873	$+_{10}+5$
8	$-07.63_{10}12$
-47	$+0.512500$
$+37.98376$	$2_{10}8$
0	$02.800_{10}-003$

The following are acceptable ways of writing the real number 200:

200	$+2_{10}+2$
$+200$	$20.0000_{10}+1$
200.0	$.0002_{10}6$
$2_{10}2$	$20000_{10}-2$

The following are *not* acceptable real numbers:

6.	(must not end in decimal point)

---

* Few present hardware representations accept this notation. In ALGOL for the Burroughs B5000, $\times 10 *$ is substituted for the lowered 10, leading to numbers like $1.258 \times 10 * 6$ and $2 \times 10 * - 9$. In an ALGOL system which follows FORTRAN notation the letter E is substituted for the lowered 10, leading to numbers like 1.258E6 and $2E - 9$.

$157._{10}7$	(must not end in decimal point, even if there is an exponent part)
$1.853 \cdot 10^5$	(the 10 must be lowered, the dot is not permitted, and the exponent must not be raised)
87,649,992	(commas not permitted)
$14.7_{10}2.5$	(exponent must be an integer)

2.2 Variables and Variable Identifiers

The term *variable* is used in ALGOL to denote any quantity that is referred to by name rather than by explicit appearance and that is able to take on different values rather than being restricted to one value.

Variables may be of the real or integer type.* An integer variable is simply one that can take on any of the values permitted of an integer number, namely zero or any positive or negative integer no greater than the limit imposed by the hardware representation. A real variable is one that can take on any of the values permitted of a real number, namely zero or any positive or negative rational number no greater or smaller than the limits imposed by the hardware representation. Real variables are also stored in most computers in a different way than integer variables are: a real variable is always stored with an exponent part that locates the decimal point. Generally, most variables in an ALGOL program will be set up as real variables because of the convenience provided by the automatic handling of decimal points. Integer variables are useful in special situations that we shall investigate later.

A *variable identifier* is a name given to a variable by the programmer. ALGOL provides almost complete flexibility in devising variable identifiers: there are no restrictions except that an identifier must begin with a letter of the alphabet and must contain only letters and digits. An identifier can be any length.

The reference and publication languages permit both lower- and upper-case letters, which are considered distinct; thus sigma, Sigma, and SIGMA are all different identifiers. Very few computers are able to accept both, however, making it necessary to use only capital letters. In this book we use both, but we never employ identifiers that are

---

* Or Boolean, as we shall see in Chapter 3.

distinguished only by upper- and lower-case letters.

The publication language permits other symbols to be used as long as they do not conflict with symbols that have special meaning in ALGOL. A typical example would be letters of the Greek alphabet.

The following are all acceptable variable identifiers:

A	DALLAS
a	largest
Alpha	diagonal
x12	B7
Gsquared	a1b2c3d4e5

The assignment of identifiers to variables is entirely under control of the programmer. Common practice is to devise names that suggest the meaning of the variable, such as $X2$ for X squared or pi for a variable that always has the value π to some number of places. It should be noted that ALGOL does not attach meaning to any characteristic of an identifier. If the programmer chooses to assign names that simplify recall of the meaning of the variable, it is perfectly permissible to do so, but no such meaning is attached to the symbols by ALGOL. A name such as $B7$ specifically is *not* interpreted by ALGOL to mean B times 7, B to the seventh power, or B_7. Furthermore, no distinction of any type is made between the rules for forming identifiers of real and integer variables. It should also be noted that every combination of letters and digits constitutes a separate identifier. Thus ABC is a different identifier from BAC, and the identifiers A, AB, and $AB7$ are all distinct.

There is one consideration that is in a sense a restriction on the free invention of identifiers. A number of words are used in ALGOL with special meaning, namely, **true, false, go to, if, then, else, for, do, step, until, while, comment, begin, end, own, Boolean, integer, real, array, switch, procedure, string, label,** and **value.** It is conventional to underline these words to set them off from identifiers; as a typographical convenience, they are shown in this book in **boldface.**

Ideally, these ALGOL words would always be represented by distinctive symbols to show that they stand for themselves and nothing else. If this were the case, the ALGOL word **true** could never be confused with the identifier true, which might be invented by a programmer. In some hardware representations ALGOL words are set off by distinguishing marks such as quotes or dollar signs, so that there is in fact no confusion between 'true' and true or between $while$ and while. In systems not having a distinguishing method it is necessary to avoid all ALGOL words as identifiers.

In any case, it is necessary to avoid use of identifiers that are the same as the identifiers of certain standard functions to be investigated shortly: abs, sign, sqrt, sin, cos, arctan, ln, exp, and entier.

2.3 Arithmetic Expressions

The idea of an *expression* appears repeatedly in ALGOL, most frequently in connection with the assignment statement by which we give a new value to a variable.

An expression is a collection of one or more numbers, variables, and functions (see Section 2.4), combined with arithmetic operators and parentheses to form a meaningful mathematical expression. Note that a single number or variable is an expression.

The common arithmetic operators and the symbols * used to denote them are

addition	$+$
subtraction	$-$
multiplication	$\times$
division	/ and sometimes $\div$
exponentiation	$\uparrow$

Examples of expressions:

$$16.48$$
$$\text{Alpha}$$
$$r \uparrow 2 - s \uparrow 2$$
$$a + b - c$$
$$\text{sumsquares}/n$$
$$(x - y - z)/(a + b)$$
$$87 \times (\text{theta} - 2 \times N)$$
$$a/(2 \times (a + b \times x) \uparrow 2)$$

An arithmetic expression always defines a single value; what is done with this value depends on where the expression is written. If it is written on the right side of an assignment statement, it causes a new value to be assigned to the variable named on the left. For example, the assignment

---

* In most hardware representations not all of these symbols are available. ALGOL for the Burroughs B5000 substitutes the letter combination DIV for $\div$ and * for $\uparrow$. Other substitutions might be * for $\times$, // for $\div$, and ** for $\uparrow$.

statement

$$Y := X + 3.69$$

causes the value of the variable Y to be replaced with the value of the variable X, plus 3.69.

Every variable named in an expression must already have been given a value, either by an earlier assignment statement or by reading in data from punched cards or magnetic tape. The value of a variable in general changes during the execution of a program. Whenever a variable name appears in an expression, it identifies the value *most recently assigned* to that variable.

Two arithmetic operators must never be written side by side. Thus, $A \times -B$ is not a legitimate expression, but $A \times (-B)$ and $-A \times B$ are. Since plus and minus signs are indistinguishable from the arithmetic operators for addition and subtraction, this rule also means that any exponent expression beginning with a sign must be enclosed in parentheses.

In the absence of parentheses to define precedence, all exponentiations are carried out first, then all multiplications and divisions, and then all additions and subtractions. Thus the following two expressions are equivalent:

$$A \times B + C/D - E \times F \uparrow G$$

$$(A \times B) + (C/D) - (E \times (F \uparrow G))$$

Naturally, one is not limited to the precedence defined by this rule: parentheses can be used to override it. Thus $(x + y)^3$ would be written $(x + y) \uparrow 3$ to convey the intended meaning; $x + y \uparrow 3$ would mean $x + y^3$. Since exponentiation is the highest ranking operation, any exponent expression other than a single unsigned number or variable must be enclosed in parentheses. For instance, the mathematical expression $\left(\dfrac{x}{10}\right)^{2i-1}$ must be written $(x/10)$ $\uparrow (2 \times i - 1)$; if it were written $(x/10) \uparrow 2 \times i - 1$, the rules of precedence would cause it to be interpreted as $\left(\dfrac{x}{10}\right)^2 \cdot i - 1$, which is not the same thing at all.

If neither parentheses nor the rules of precedence define the sequence of operations, they are carried out from left to right. Thus $A/B \times C$ means $\dfrac{A}{B} \cdot C$, not $\dfrac{A}{B \cdot C}$, and $2 \uparrow 2 \uparrow k$ means $(2^2)^k$, not $2^{(2^k)}$. It may be seen that this left-to-right assumption defines the meaning of expressions that are con-

sidered ambiguous in ordinary mathematical notation, such as $A/B \times C$.

The multiplication sign must never be omitted, as it frequently is in ordinary mathematical notation. It is easy to see why this rule must be followed: without it, there would be no way to determine whether AB meant A times B or the single variable named AB.

This sort of consideration can occasionally have a bearing on the computation of expressions that in ordinary mathematical notation are considered equivalent, when large and/or small numbers are involved. Suppose that A and B are large and nearly equal and that C is small in the expression $A - B + C$. Taken from *left to right*, this means $(A - B) + C$, which first subtracts one large number from another, giving a small number, and then adds a small number. If the expression were taken from *right to left*, the expression would mean to subtract a large number from a small number and then add a large number. The difficulty is that if B were a great deal larger than C subtracting them could cause complete loss of significance in C, so that the two interpretations of the expression would not give the same result, even though they were mathematically equivalent. (Try both versions on $12345.678 - 12345.678 + 0.00012345678$, *discarding all but eight significant digits after each operation*.)

Real and integer quantities may be mixed freely in an expression. For the operators $+$, $-$, and $\times$, the value of the expression will be integer if both operands are of type integer, and real otherwise. The operator $/$ is defined for all four combinations of operands of type real and integer and yields a quotient of type real in any case.

There is a special division operator $\div$, defined only if both operands are the integer type. The result is always type integer and is found by *truncating* the quotient; that is, there is no rounding. Stated otherwise, this operator gives the *integer* quotient of two integers, and the remainder is ignored. Thus $7 \div 4$ gives 1, not 2, and $99 \div 100$ equals zero. In applications of this operator the truncation aspect requires careful attention to the sequence of operations. For instance, $6 \times 4 \div 3$ gives 8; 6 is multiplied by 4, giving 24, which is divided by 3 to give 8. However, if the expression is written $6 \times (4 \div 3)$, the result will be 6: the parentheses force the division to be done first, giving the integer 1 (no rounding, remember), which is multiplied by 6 to produce 6.

Mathematical Notation	Correct Expression	Incorrect Expression
$A \cdot B$	$A \times B$	AB (No operator)
$A \cdot (-B)$	$A \times (-B)$ or $-A \times B$	$A \times -B$ (Two operators side by side)
$-(A + B)$	$-(A + B)$	$-A + B$ or $-+A + B$
A^{i+2}	$A \uparrow (i + 2)$	$A \uparrow i + 2 (= A^i + 2)$
$A^{j-3} \cdot B$	$A \uparrow (j - 3) \times B$	$A \uparrow j - 3 \times B (= A^j - 3B)$
$\dfrac{A \cdot B}{C \cdot D}$	$A \times B/(C \times D)$ or $A/C \times B/D$	$A \times B/C \times D \left(= \dfrac{ABD}{C}\right)$
$\left(\dfrac{A + B}{C}\right)^{2.5}$	$((A + B)/C) \uparrow 2.5$	$(A + B)/C \uparrow 2.5 \left(= \dfrac{A + B}{C^{2.5}}\right)$
$A[X + B(X + C)]$	$A \times (X + B \times (X + C))$	$A(X + B(X + C))$
$(-A)^i$	$(-A) \uparrow i$	$-A \uparrow i (= -(A^i))$

Figure 2.1. Correct and incorrect ALGOL expressions.

This operator is obviously of a rather special nature, to be used only when there is a specific need for its features. The foregoing examples illustrate nicely how careful one must be when working with a computer to be positive that the processing is carried out precisely as intended.

The operator $\uparrow$ produces various kinds of results, depending on the size and type of the base and of the exponent. Denote a number of the integer type by i, a number of the real type by r, and a number of either type by a. Then the meaning of the exponentiation operator is given by the following rules:

$a \uparrow i$ If $i > 0$, $a \times a \times \ldots \times a$ (i times), of the same type as a.
  If $i = 0$, if $a \neq 0$, 1, of the same type as a.
    if $a = 0$, undefined.
  If $i < 0$, if $a \neq 0$, $1/(a \times a \times \ldots \times a)$ (the denominator has $-i$ factors), of type real.
    if $a = 0$, undefined.

$a \uparrow r$ If $a > 0$, $\exp(r \times \ln(a))$, of type real, i.e., $e^{r \ln a}$.
  If $a = 0$, if $r > 0$, 0.0, of type real.
    if $r \leq 0$, undefined.
  If $a < 0$, always undefined.

Figure 2.1 illustrates some correct and incorrect ways of forming ALGOL expressions to correspond to mathematical expressions.

2.4 Common Functions

ALGOL provides a simple mechanism for the use of certain common mathematical functions such as square root, sine, and absolute value. All we need do is write the name of the function desired; the ALGOL processor will automatically incorporate the machine language instructions to compute the function. The argument for which we want the function value is written in parentheses following the function name.

The number and kind of functions that may be included in a program automatically vary generally with the processor and the computer installation, but certain common ones are available in just about every system. These standard functions and their identifiers are

abs (E)	the absolute value of the value of the arithmetic expression E.
sign (E)	the sign function of the value of E $= \begin{cases} +1 \text{ if E} > 0 \\ 0 \text{ if E} = 0 \\ -1 \text{ if E} < 0. \end{cases}$
sqrt (E)	the square root of the value of E.
sin (E)	the sine of the value of E, E assumed to be expressed in radians.*
cos (E)	the cosine of the value of E, E assumed to be expressed in radians.*
arctan (E)	the principal value of the arctangent of the value of E, produced in radians.*
ln (E)	the natural logarithm of the value of E.*
exp (E)	the exponential function of the value of E, that is, e^E, where e is the base of the natural logarithms.*
entier (E)	the largest integer not greater than the value of E.†

---

* A few conversion formulas may be stated for reference.

$$E \text{ degrees} = 0.01745329 \text{ E radians}$$
$$E \text{ radians} = 57.29578 \text{ E degrees}$$
$$\log E = 0.43429448 \ln E$$
$$\ln E = 2.3025851 \log E$$
$$10^E = \exp (2.3025851 \text{ E})$$

† Roughly speaking, "entier" is French for "entire." In mathematics entier (E) is commonly called the *greatest integer function* of E and is written [E].

In every case the expression in parentheses may be any arithmetic expression. Writing the function name, followed by parentheses enclosing an expression, calls for the evaluation of the named function of the expression.

2.5 The Assignment Statement

An ALGOL *statement* is an order to perform some action. As we shall see, an ALGOL program is composed of a series of statements of various kinds, including some that specify the sequence of execution of other statements.

The fundamental statement is the *assignment* statement, which assigns a value to one or more variables. A simple assignment statement takes the form

$$\text{Variable} := \text{Expression}$$

This is not an equation! It is instead a command: *replace* the value of the variable on the left with the value of the expression on the right. The combination $:=$ is sometimes called the *replacement operator;* it is not a statement of equality. The reference language uses the combination of the colon and the equal sign to denote replacement and reserves the ordinary equal sign for use as a *relational* operator, as we shall see in Chapter . A good policy is to think of $:=$ as meaning "is placed by."

Examples of assignment statements:

x := 3	replace the present value of x with the value 3.
omega := theta + 6.2832	replace the present value of omega with the value of theta p
deriv := N × cos (ang) ↑ (N − 1)	replace the present value of *deriv* with the value of Nc where the current values of N and of *ang* are to be use ing the expression.
k := k − 1	compute the value of $k − 1$, using the current val computation, then replace the current value of k of the expression just computed. In short, decreas

This last example, which is clearly not an equation, brings out rather forcefully that $:=$ means is replaced by, not *equals*.

The examples in Figure 2.2 show several ordinary formulas and corresponding assignment statements. Identifiers of variables have been chosen to suggest the original quantities, but the choices, of course, are arbitrary; any other identifiers would have been just as acceptable to ALGOL. It is also assumed that previous statements would have assigned values to all the variables on the right.

It is permissible for the variable on the left to be of the real type and the expression on the right to be of the integer type, and vice versa. In such a case the expression on the right is evaluated in the type of arithmetic dictated by its variables and operators; then the value of the expression is converted to the type of the variable on the left. In most computers real and integer variables are stored somewhat differently, so that a conversion in the form of representation is required. In any case, an assignment statement of the form *integer*

$:= real$ will cause the value of the real expression to be rounded to an integer. This feature is occasionally useful in itself.

A single assignment statement can set several variables equal to the same value by a simple and obvious extension of the notation. For instance, if x, y, and z are all to be made zero, we can write

$$x := y := z := 0$$

All "left part" variables must be of the same type.

Seldom will anything complicated be done with such a multiple assignment statement, but a complete definition must account for certain unusual possibilities. One is that the expression at the right of the statement involves one of the variables in the list of variables to be assigned new values. The procedure is this: the expression on the right is evaluated, using the current values of all variables appearing in it; all variables in the list are then assigned this value. Consider the statement

$$a := b := c := c + 1$$

Original Mathematical Formula	ALGOL Assignment Statement
$R = \dfrac{A + BX}{C + DX}$	R := (A + B × X)/(C + D × X)
$\beta = \dfrac{-1}{2X} + \dfrac{A^2}{4X^2}$	Beta := −1/(2 × X) + A ↑ 2/(4 × X ↑ 2)
$F_y = X \dfrac{X^2 - Y^2}{X^2 + Y^2}$	Fy := X × (X ↑ 2 − Y ↑ 2)/(X ↑ 2 + Y ↑ 2)
$C = 1.112K \dfrac{r_1 r_2}{r_1 - r_2}$	C := 1.112 × K × r1 × r2/(r1 − r2)
$J = 4K - 6k_1 k_2$	J := 4 × K − 6 × k1 × k2
$k = 12$	k := 12
$\pi = 3.1415927$	pi := 3.1415927
$I = \dfrac{x}{a} - \dfrac{1}{ap} \ln(a + be^{px})$	I := x/a − 1/(a × p) × ln (a + b × exp (p × x))
$V = \dfrac{1}{m\sqrt{ab}} \tan^{-1}\left(e^{mx}\sqrt{\dfrac{a}{b}}\right)$	V := 1/(m × sqrt (a × b)) × arctan (exp (m × x) × sqrt (a/b))
$M_{new} = 2M_{old} + 10J$	M := 2 × M + 10 × J
$I_{new} = I_{old} + 1$	I := I + 1
$I_{new} = nI_{old}$	I := n × I
$I_{new} = I_{old}^2$	I := I ↑ 2

Figure 2.2. Some formulas and corresponding ALGOL assignment statements.

Incorrect Statement	Error
$Y := 2X + A$	$\times$ missing
$3.14 := x - a$	Left side must be a variable
$gamma := 1,678,982 \times delta$	Commas not allowed in constants
$a := ((x + y)a \uparrow 2 + (R - s) \uparrow 2/16.8$	Not same number of left and right parentheses; $\times$ missing
$-m := i \uparrow 4$	Variable on left must not be written with a sign
$a \times x \uparrow 2 + b \times x + c := 0$	Left side must be a single variable

Figure 2.3. Some errors in writing assignment statements.

This means to add 1 to the present value of c and then make c, b, and a equal to the sum.

There is really nothing very difficult about writing ALGOL assignment statements. For the most part the rules are those of familiar mathematical notation. There *are* a few restrictions, however. To emphasize some of the things commonly forgotten by beginners, Figure 2.3 illustrates some errors in writing assignment statements.

EXERCISES

*1. Do the following pairs of ALGOL real numbers represent the same number in each case?

16.9	$+16.9$
23000	$2.3_{10}4$
0.000007	$.7_{10} - 5$
1.0	1.000
$.906_{10}5$	$+906.000_{10} + 2$

*2. Which of the following are acceptable variable identifiers?

X	i12g	Cat	$x + 3$	next
42Y	delta	A/M	Last	T1.4
(square)	IA	AI	x	X12
1X2	xsquared	arctan	begin	while
2a	g^{-1}	158	First Bessel function	
set	next1	Lasted	T1point4	B$_7$

3. Write ALGOL arithmetic expressions corresponding to each of the following mathematical expressions:

a. $x + y^3$ b. $(x + y)^3$

* c. $x^{1.667}$ d. $A + \dfrac{B}{C}$

e. $\dfrac{A + B}{C}$ * f. $A + \dfrac{B}{C + D}$

g. $\dfrac{A + B}{C + D}$ * h. $\dfrac{A + B}{C + D} + X_1^2$

* i. $\dfrac{A + B}{C + \dfrac{D}{F + G}}$ * j. $1 + x + \dfrac{x^{~}}{2!} + \dfrac{x^3}{3!}$

k. $\left(\dfrac{p_1}{p_2}\right)^{g-1}$ * l. $\dfrac{x}{1 + \dfrac{x^2}{3 + \dfrac{(2x)^2}{5 + \dfrac{(3x)^2}{7 + (4x)^2}}}}$

* m. $a \cdot b + c^d - (2^x)^2$ n. $(x_1^3 + x_2^3 + x_3^3)$

o. $AREA = 2 \cdot P \cdot R \cdot \sin(\pi/P)$

p. $CHORD = 2R \sin \dfrac{A}{2}$

q. $ARC = 2\sqrt{Y^2 + (4X^2/3)}$

r. $S = -\dfrac{\cos^4 X}{4}$

4. Shown below are a number of mathematical expressions and corresponding ALGOL arithmetic expressions. All contain at least one error. Point out the errors and write correct expressions.

a. $(x + y)^3$ $x + y \uparrow 3$

* b. $\dfrac{x + 2}{y + 4}$ $x + 2/y + 4$

c. $\dfrac{A \cdot B}{C + 2}$ $AB/(C + 2)$

* d. $\left(\dfrac{X + A + \pi}{2Z}\right)^2$ $(X + A + 3.1416)$ $/(2 \times Z) \uparrow 2$

e. $\left(\dfrac{X}{Y}\right)^{n-1}$ $(X/Y) \uparrow n - 1$

* f. $\dfrac{a}{b} + \dfrac{c \cdot d}{e \cdot f \cdot g}$ $a/b + cd/efg$

g. $(m + n)(r + s)$ $m + n \times r + s$

h. $a + bx + cx^2 + dx^3$
$= a + x [b + x (c + dx)]$ $\qquad$ $a + x \times (b + x \times (c + d \times x)$

*i. $\dfrac{1{,}600{,}042 \cdot G + 10^5}{4{,}568{,}995 \cdot G + 10^5}$ $\qquad$ $(1{,}600{,}042 \times G + 1._{10}5)/(4{,}568{,}995 \times G + 1.10^5)$

j. $\left(\dfrac{1}{A}\right)^2 \cdot \left(\dfrac{R}{12.3}\right)^3 \cdot \left(\dfrac{2S}{23.4}\right)^4$ $\qquad$ $1/A \uparrow 2 \times (R/12.3) \uparrow 3 \times (2S/23.4) \uparrow 4$

5. The following expressions are all acceptable, but each contains at least one pair of parentheses that can be removed without changing the meaning of the expression. Rewrite the expressions with the minimum number of parentheses. (There is nothing really wrong with extra parentheses, of course. In fact, they are often advisable, just to make the meaning clearer.)

a. $(A \times B)/C$
b. $(A/B) \times C$
c. $(A + X) \times (B/Y)$
*d. $(A + B \uparrow (i + 2) \times (B/C))$
e. $(A \times B \times C)/(D \times E)$
*f. $(a \times (b/(c \times (d/(e \times f)))))$
g. $(a \uparrow (i + 2) + b \uparrow (i + 3) + (X + 4) \times (b)))$
h. $(A \uparrow (i - j + 1))/(A \uparrow (i - j + 1) + 6.28)$
*i. $(((A) + (B)) + (C) \times (D) \uparrow 2)/(((A + 7.9) \uparrow (i - 1) + B/(C + D)) \times (A + 6))$
j. $(((((A/B) \times C)/D) \times R) + (A/(S \uparrow K)) - (((B \uparrow 2) \times T)/(W \uparrow 4)))$

3. PROGRAM ORGANIZATION, if-STATEMENTS, AND BOOLEAN VARIABLES

3.1 Elements of Program Organization

An ALGOL program is composed largely of *statements,* a statement being a command to perform some action. We saw in Chapter 2 that an *assignment statement* causes a new value to be assigned to one or more variables. We shall see that there are several other kinds of statements, some of which are considerably more flexible than the assignment statement.

The statements of a program are executed sequentially as written, in the absence of instructions to the contrary. However, this one-after-the-other sequence may be interrupted in several ways, of which two are considered in this chapter: The *go to statement* explicitly names the statement to be executed next, and the *if-statement* permits statements to be executed in a sequence that depends on the values of data and results.

Because of this possibility of *transfer of control* (nonsequential execution of instructions), and for other reasons, it is necessary to specify precisely where every statement ends. For this purpose, every statement must be followed either by a semicolon,* the word **end,** or the word **else.** Which of the three to use is determined by rules that will

---

* Many computers require a transliteration of the semicolon; a simple and common substitution is the dollar sign.

be considered later; the semicolon is most common.

It is often desirable to make a number of statements act as a single group for purposes that we shall begin to investigate shortly. In such a case the group must be preceded by the word **begin** and followed by the word **end;** the group is then called a *compound statement.* The words **begin** and **end** are called *statement parentheses,* since they serve to denote the limits of a group of statements in much the same way as ordinary parentheses specify the limits of a mathematical expression that is to be treated as a unit in later operations. A semicolon is not necessary before the **end.**

A *block* has the appearance of a compound statement, being enclosed between **begin** and **end,** but in addition it includes *declarations* immediately following the **begin.** There are various kinds of declarations, which we shall investigate in subsequent chapters; at a minimum, every variable must be declared to be of type **real, integer,** or **Boolean.** (Boolean variables are discussed in Section 3.6.) For many simple programs the only declaration required is the word **real** followed by the identifiers of all variables in the program.

Every program must be a block; that is, it must start with **begin,** be followed by declarations and the statements of the program, and terminate with **end.** Thus we

```
            begin real E, R, L, C, I, F;
            Read (E, R, L, C);
            Print (E, R, L, C);
Repeat:     Read (F);
            I := E/sqrt (R ↑ 2 + (6.2832 × F × L − 1/(6.2832 × F × C)) ↑ 2);
            Print (F, I);
            go to Repeat
            end
```

Figure 3.1. An ALGOL program to read a data card, compute a result, and return to read another card.

now see that Figure 1.5 was not a complete ALGOL program. We shall see in Chapter 6 that block structure does a good deal more than merely setting the boundaries of a program.

3.2 Labels and the go to Statement

In order for one statement to refer to another, it is necessary to be able to identify a statement, which is the purpose of *labels*. A label may be any unsigned integer or it may be any identifier, which, it will be recalled, is a string of letters and digits beginning with a letter. A label must always be followed by a colon * to separate it from the statement that it precedes.

ALGOL attaches no meaning to the arrangement of statements in a program, except for their sequence. Blank spaces may be freely inserted into statements to improve readability, and statements may be arranged into lines in any way that the programmer wishes. One line may contain one statement, several statements, or only part of a statement. Readability (by a human, that is) is considerably enhanced by some systematic format, such as putting each statement on a separate line and by some scheme of indentation that clarifies relationships within the program.

The go to statement is about the simplest in the language. It is of the general form **go to** L, where L is the label of a statement elsewhere in the program. It specifies that the statement to be executed next is the one identified by the label.

A particularly simple usage of the go to statement is to return from the end of a program to its beginning, to execute it again. The following example illustrates this application of the statement and also shows how an ALGOL program can be organized on the page.

* One simple transliteration of the colon is two periods.

Suppose that we are required to compute the current flowing in an a-c circuit containing resistance, capacitance, and inductance. The steady-state current in a series circuit of this type is given by

$$I = \frac{E}{\sqrt{R^2 + \left(2\pi FL - \dfrac{1}{2\pi FC}\right)^2}}$$

where I = current, amperes
      E = voltage, volts
      R = resistance, ohms
      L = inductance, henrys
      C = capacitance, farads
      F = frequency, cycles per second

We assume that the purpose of the computation is to provide the data for drawing a graph of the relation between current and frequency for fixed values of voltage, resistance, inductance, and capacitance. The fixed values of these variables are read from a card at the beginning of the program. The desired values of frequency are read from a series of cards; after each card is read, the current for that frequency is computed and printed.

An ALGOL program to do this job is shown in Figure 3.1. Reading this program should present no difficulty, but a few additional words should be said about the purpose of some of its features. A printed report can be almost useless without some identification in addition to the answers. Therefore, a Print statement has been placed after the Read, to print the values of voltage, resistance, inductance, and capacitance as soon as they have been read. For the same reason, each current value is printed with the corresponding frequency. There is no provision for stopping the execution of this program; it will therefore continue reading frequency cards, computing the current, printing it, and returning to read another frequency card as long as cards remain to be read. When the last card has been read, the computer will "hang up" trying to read another card. This is usually not good practice, at least on large computers; another approach is presented in Section 3.3.

Note that no semicolon is required after the go to statement, since it is immediately followed by the word **end.** See the rule at the end of Section 3.1.

It may be well at this point to review the procedure for setting an ALGOL program into operation.

1. The program is written approximately as shown in Figure 3.1, except that it is written on some kind of form that makes the desired spacing more explicit, and any transliterations required by the particular hardware representation are made. In most present computers only capital letters may be used.

2. The program is punched onto cards or paper tape (and perhaps transcribed from there onto magnetic tape). The result is the *source program* deck (or tape). It does *not* include data cards.

3. The ALGOL processor, which is itself a large program of computer instructions, is read into the machine from another deck of cards or, more commonly, from magnetic tape or from magnetic drum.

4. The processor reads the source program deck or tape, *not* including any data cards, into the computer and *compiles* it into an *object program* consisting of actual machine instructions. Depending on the circumstances, the object program may be left in the machine ready to run or it may be written out onto cards or tape. *The object program has not been executed and no data cards have been read.*

5. The processor program is removed from the scene and the object program takes over after being read in from cards or tape if it was not left in the machine by the processor. With the computer under control of the object program, the machine instructions produced from the source program can carry out the specified processing, including reading of data and printing of results.

It is important that this process be clearly understood; much of the following material would be almost meaningless without such an understanding. This is all the more true because of the short cuts that must be taken to describe the operation of programs. The phrase "the execution of the machine instructions produced from the statement in the source program" is awkward if repeated as often as would be necessary. We therefore use such phrases as "when the if-statement is executed." It must never be forgotten that this is an abbreviation for the complete phrase; the actual execution occurs only *after* compilation.

In some ALGOL systems the translation of the source program to an object program is done so unobtrusively that one may not quite realize that it has happened. This is the case if the translation is very fast and the object program is left in the computer ready to run, in which case it may be customary to place the data cards immediately following the source program. Except for a short delay after reading the source program, it might *appear* that the source program is being executed as soon as it is read, but this is not so.

The reader who wishes to get ahead of the game and try some programs on a computer at this point, which is an excellent idea, should bear in mind that virtually every processor requires some transliterations, such as replacing ↑ with * or **. Check the manual for your system. Also check the manual for the simplest possible way to write input and output statements; it is quite unlikely that the simplified statements in this book will be acceptable. In most cases you will have to add some kind of specification of the format of the cards and of the printed report, but do not try to do anything fancy. If there is some simplified form of input and output requiring no format information, by all means use it.

3.3 The if-Statement

The go to statement provides a way to alter the sequence of statement execution *unconditionally.* Besides this, however, we need a way to change the sequence of statement execution *on the basis of what happens during execution of the program.* In other words, we need a way of making a *conditional* transfer of control based on data or computed results. The *if-statement* provides this capability, among other things.

A few definitions will simplify the explanation of the if-statement. A *relational operator* is any of the following: $<$, $\leq$, $=$, $\geq$, $>$, or $\neq$. Note that the equal sign is written here without a colon. The relational operator $=$ is to be interpreted in the sense, "if one arithmetic expression is equal to another arithmetic expression, then the relation is

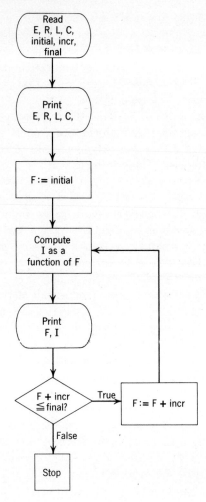

Figure 3.2. Block diagram of a program to compute current in an a-c circuit for equally spaced values of frequency.

The if-statement is easily described in terms of these definitions. In its simplest version the general form of this statement is

if relation **then** statement

The operation is as follows: if the relation is true, the statement following **then** is executed; if the relation is false, the statement following **then** is not executed and control passes to the next statement in sequence.

For example, the if-statement

if x $<$ 10 **then go to** delta;

will cause a transfer to the statement having the label delta if x is less than 10; if x is greater than or equal to 10, the entire statement will have no effect and control will pass on to the statement that follows.

The statement following the **then** can be of any type except another conditional. Frequently it will be a compound statement, as in the following example:

if F + incr $\leq$ final **then begin**

$$F := F + incr; \textbf{go to} \text{ repeat } \textbf{end}$$

The **begin** and **end,** we recall, are statement brackets denoting the limits of a compound statement. They are essential here, incidentally. Without them, the action would be correct as long as the relation is true, but as soon as it becomes false the effect would be to skip over the F : = F + incr and continue to the go to statement. The effect is thus quite different from what it is with the brackets, in which case *both* statements between **begin** and **end** are skipped when the relation is false.

This example provides the basis for a much more realistic version of the example in Section 3.2. Suppose that instead of reading every new value of frequency from a card we read just three numbers from a card at the beginning. These are the first frequency, named *initial*, an increment, named *incr*, and a largest value, named *final*. The pattern is now to be as follows: compute the current for the initial frequency, then increment the frequency repeatedly and compute the current for each new value, but stop the process as soon as the current has been computed for the largest value of frequency not exceeding the final value.

As usual, a block diagram is easier to follow than a verbal description. Figure 3.2 shows the procedure clearly. The precise nature of the test

true." On the other hand, the separator : = means to assign the value of the expression on its right to the variable(s) on its left and has nothing to do with the idea of equality. This distinction between the equal sign as a replacement operator and the equal sign as a relational operator is not always made clear in elementary mathematics; it must be made explicit in any algorithmic language.

A *relation* is of the form E_1RE_2 where E_1 and E_2 are any two arithmetic expressions and R is any relational operator. A relation is said to be *true* or *false,* depending on whether the relation is satisfied by the values of the expressions. A relation should therefore not be thought of as a statement of fact but rather as an assertion that may be true or false. For instance, the relation $x = 2$ does not mean that x equals 2 but rather, in effect, asks, "Is it true that x is equal to 2?"

begin real E, R, L, C, I, F, initial, incr, final;
Read (E, R, L, C, initial, incr, final);
Print (E, R, L, C);
F : = initial;
twopi : = 6.2831853;
Repeat: I : = E/sqrt(R ↑ 2 + (twopi × F × L − 1/(twopi × F × C)) ↑ 2);
Print (F, I);
if F + incr ≦ final **then begin** F : = F + incr; **go to** Repeat **end;**
Stop
end

Figure 3.3. An ALGOL program to carry out the computation diagrammed in Figure 3.2.

is worth noting. We ask, in effect, "Would adding the increment once more give a new frequency less than or equal to the specified final value?" If the answer is yes (true), we go ahead and add the increment and repeat the computation of the current. If the answer is no (false), we stop the process.

An ALGOL program is shown in Figure 3.3. There is nothing really new here, except the Stop. This is not an ALGOL statement, as Read and Print are not; all three would have to be defined as procedures, as discussed in Chapter 7. Note also the assignment of the value 6.2831853 to the variable named *twopi*, to avoid having to write out the long constant twice. This is common practice.

3.4 The Conditional Statement

The if-statement, as we have defined it so far, provides for carrying out a statement if and only if some relation is true. Stated otherwise, it provides for skipping over a statement if some relation is false. A complete conditional statement does more; it specifies a second statement to be carried out if and only if the relation is *false*. The general form is:

if relation **then** S_1 **else** S_2;

where S_1 and S_2 are any two statements. The operation is as follows: if the relation is true, statement S_1 is executed and statement S_2 is skipped; if the relation is false, statement S_1 is skipped and statement S_2 is executed. In either case control passes to whatever statement follows S_2 (unless S_1 or S_2 contain go to statements).

For an example, suppose that at a certain point

in a program we must do the following. If $t = n − 1$, set D equal to x^2 and go on to what follows, but if $t \neq n − 1$ go to the statement labeled *special*. This can be done with the statement:

if t = n − 1 **then** D : = x ↑ 2 **else go to** special;

The following statement has exactly the same result:

if t ≠ n − 1 **then go to** special **else** D : = x ↑ 2;

This last statement, in turn, has the same effect as the two statements:

if t ≠ n − 1 **then go to** special;

D : = x ↑ 2;

In the general form of the conditional statement the statement following **then** must be unconditional, but there is no such restriction on the statement following **else**. It may very well be another conditional statement. Conditional statements can be "nested" in this way to any depth. A nest of two conditionals, for instance, would appear in skeleton form as

if R_1 **then** S_1 **else if** R_2 **then** S_2 **else** S_3; S_4

The word **else** implies two actions. The obvious one is to indicate what to do if a preceding relation is not true; in this sense, it means "otherwise." The other function is to dictate what to do if a preceding relation *is* true. The word **else** always occurs in the combination

then S **else**

where it *defines the successor of statement S as the statement following the entire conditional statement* (unless S is or includes a go to statement, of course). In schematic block diagram form the nest above can be expressed as shown in Figure 3.4.

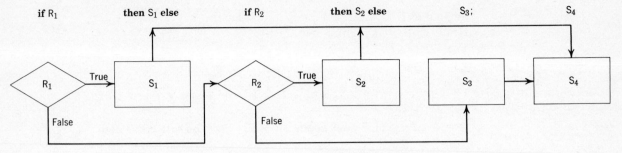

Figure 3.4. Schematic block diagram of the meaning of a "nested" conditional statement.

The effect of this construction can be stated another way: the statement is inspected from left to right; as soon as a relation that is true is found, the unconditional statement following it is executed and the rest of the conditional is skipped entirely; if all relations are false, the statement following the last **else** (if there is one) is executed. If all relations are false and there is no **else** at the end, the entire statement has no effect.

All of this may be illustrated with the following hypothetical example. We are given these specifications:

1. If $a < b$, set g equal to 8.9 and go on.

2. If $alpha - beta \geq 14.7$, set rho equal to cos $(theta/2)$, set $sigma$ equal to $7 - tau^{1.5}$ and go on to whatever follows these steps.

3. If neither of the above is true, go to the statement labeled $unusual$, which is somewhere else—not shown here.

4. After executing the statements in (1) or (2), set $flag$ equal to 1.

All this can be done with the following:

if a < b **then** g : = 8.9 **else**
if alpha − beta $\geq$ 14.7 **then**
begin
rho : = cos (theta/2);
sigma : = 7 − tau ↑ 1.5 **end**
else go to unusual;
flag : = 1;

3.5 The if-Clause

We have so far discussed the if-then-else construction in terms of its use as a complete statement. The same general form can be applied in a variety of ways by relaxing the assumption that complete statements are involved. The generalization is almost obvious. Suppose, for example,

we wish to set $signal$ equal to zero if $w = z$ and set it equal to 1 otherwise. This can be done with the single assignment statement:

$$signal : = \textbf{if } w = z \textbf{ then } 0 \textbf{ else } 1;$$

This has exactly the same effect as the complete if-statement:

$$\textbf{if } w = z \textbf{ then } signal : = 0 \textbf{ else } signal : = 1;$$

This explicit form is not recommended, however. The if-clause in an arithmetic expression is more compact, easier to read once the scheme is clear, and in many cases will lead to a more efficient object program.

For a second example, consider this requirement:

$$Y = 0.5X + 0.95 \text{ if } X \leq 2.1$$
$$Y = 0.7X + 0.53 \text{ if } X > 2.1$$

This computation can be specified with the concise statement:

$$Y : = \textbf{if } X \leq 2.1 \textbf{ then } 0.5 \times X + 0.95$$
$$\textbf{else } 0.7 \times X + 0.53;$$

A third example of this powerful technique involves the definite integral: *

$$Q = \int_0^\infty \frac{a\,dx}{a^2 + x^2} = \begin{cases} -\dfrac{\pi}{2} & \text{if } a < 0 \\ 0 & \text{if } a = 0 \\ +\dfrac{\pi}{2} & \text{if } a > 0 \end{cases}$$

Suppose that a has been assigned a value by a previous statement and that Q is to be found:

$$Q : = \textbf{if } a < 0 \textbf{ then } -1.5708 \textbf{ else}$$
$$\textbf{if } a = 0 \textbf{ then } 0 \textbf{ else } 1.5708;$$

* The example can be read without knowledge of calculus.

An if-clause may also be utilized in connection with a go to in another rather obvious extension of the same basic scheme. Suppose that at a certain point in a program we wish to go to the statement labeled *done* if the absolute value of the difference between x and *final* is less than 10^{-5} and otherwise to the statement labeled *more*. One statement will do it:

go to if abs (x − final) $<_{10}-5$ **then** done **else** more;

3.6   Boolean Variables and Expressions

We now turn to a generalization of the ideas contained in the discussions of relations. We saw that a relation is an assertion about two arithmetic expressions, which may be true or false. Actually, a relation is just one example of a *Boolean* * *expression,* which is closely analogous to an arithmetic expression, except that it may have only **true** or **false** as "values."

We saw that arithmetic expressions are made up of numbers, variables, and functions, combined with arithmetic operators and parentheses. Boolean expressions are formed in an analogous way from one or more of the following:

Logical values, that is, **true** or **false.**

Boolean variables, that is, variables that have been declared to be the Boolean type.

Boolean functions, that is, functions that have been declared to be the Boolean type.

Relations, as previously discussed.

These elements are called *Boolean primaries.* Any Boolean expression, even though it may be more complex than the rather simple forms permitted of a primary, may be made into a primary simply by enclosing it in parentheses. Parentheses may thus be used in the familiar manner to indicate grouping.

These primaries may be combined into more complex Boolean expressions by the use of *logical operators,* of which there are five in ALGOL.

The simplest logical operator is ⌐, which stands for *negation.* This operator always applies to a single primary; that is, it is a *unary* operator. If B

* After the English mathematician George Boole, 1815–1864, who originated the systematic study of logic as a mathematical discipline.

is any Boolean primary, then ⌐B is false if B is true, and ⌐B is true if B is false. Negation is thus similar to the unary arithmetic operator −, which reverses the sign of an arithmetic primary.

The operator ∧ is called *logical and.* If $b1$ and $b2$ are any two Boolean primaries, then $b1 ∧ b2$ is true if $b1$ and $b2$ are both true and false otherwise.

The operator ∨ is called *logical or.* If $b1$ or $b2$ *or both* are true, then $b1 ∨ b2$ is true; $b1 ∨ b2$ is false only if $b1$ and $b2$ are both false.

The logical operator ⊃ is called *implication.* If $b1$ is true and $b2$ is false, then $b1 ⊃ b2$ is false; $b1 ⊃ b2$ is true otherwise.

The logical operator ≡ is called *equivalence.* If $b1$ and $b2$ are both true or both false, $b1 ≡ b2$ is true; it is false otherwise. Implication and equivalence will have little application in the examples in this text.

It may be helpful to summarize the meaning of these operators in a *truth table,* as shown in Table 3.1.

A Boolean variable can be given a value by an assignment statement; the only requirement is that the expression on the right be a *Boolean* expression. Thus we can write statements like the following:

A : = **true**;

B : = **false**;

C : = x < 10;

The last will result in setting C equal to **true** if the current value of x is less than 10 and setting it equal to **false** otherwise.

$$D := y = 1 ∧ g > 8;$$

This will cause D to be set equal to **true** if y equals 1 *and* g is greater than 8, and will set D equal to **false** otherwise.

For further examples, suppose that the following assignment statements, in which the first four variables are obviously Boolean and the others are real, have been executed.

E : = **true**; F : = **false**; G : = **true**; H : = **true**;

R : = 2; S : = 6; T : = 0; U : = 20;

TABLE 3.1

$b1$	$b2$	⌐$b1$	$b1 ∧ b2$	$b1 ∨ b2$	$b1 ≡ b2$	$b1 ⊃ b2$
False	False	True	False	False	True	True
False	True	True	False	True	False	True
True	False	False	False	True	False	False
True	True	False	True	True	True	True

TABLE 3.2

Assignment Statement	Logical Value Assigned
L:= F;	false
M:= S ≦ T;	false
N:= H ∧ U < 25;	true
O:= ¬F ∨ R + S = T;	true
P:= G ≡ T + 12 > U;	false
Q:= E ∨ F ⊃ R = T;	false

Table 3.2 shows what values would be assigned to Boolean variables as the result of executing a number of Boolean assignment statements.

These examples raise a question that must be answered in any scheme involving a set of operators: when two or more operators appear in the same expression and the sequence is not specified by parentheses, what is the order in which the operations are performed? This is answered by stating the *hierarchy* of the operators, in our case, as follows: ¬, ∧, ∨, ⊃, ≡. In other words, in the absence of parentheses to dictate the sequence negation is performed first, then *and*, then *or*, then implication, then equivalence.

The complete definition of an if-clause may now be given; it is any construction of the form

if Boolean expression **then**

This construction may be used everywhere that we have previously used the construction

if Relation **then**

For instance, suppose we wish to stop some computational process as soon as *g* and *h* are *both* less than 0.001 in absolute value. This can be done with one statement:

if abs(g) < 0.001 ∧ abs(h) < 0.001 **then go to** exit;

For another example, suppose that a special computation must be carried out if *a* or *b* or *c* is zero:

if a = 0 ∨ b = 0 ∨ c = 0 **then go to** special;

Again, suppose that we should stop if *a* = 0 *and* *b* = 1, or *a* = 0 *and* *c* = 2. This can be done with

if a = 0 ∧ b = 1 ∨ a = 0 ∧ c = 2 **then go to** finish;

And is a higher ranking operator than *or*, so that there is no question of the meaning of this expression.

Following the maxim "when in doubt parenthesize," we could write equivalently

if (a = 0 ∧ b = 1) ∨ (a = 0 ∧ c = 2) **then go to** finish;

It happens that *and* is distributive over *or* (a fact that will not be proved here), so that we could also write

if a = 0 ∧ (b = 1 ∨ c = 2) **then go to** finish;

For an example of negation, suppose that we wish to go to *move* as long as *a* and *b* are *not both* less than 1. This can be done in several equivalent ways.

if ¬ (a < 1 ∧ b < 1) **then go to** move;

The parentheses are essential to make the unary operator ¬ apply to the entire expression. This statement may be read, "if it is not true that *a* is less than 1 and *b* is less than 1, then go to *move*."

if ¬ a < 1 ∨ ¬ b < 1 **then go to** move;

This may be read, "if it is not true that *a* is less than 1, *or* if it is not true that *b* is less than 1, then go to *move*."

if a ≧ 1 ∨ b ≧ 1 **then go to** move;

This may be read, "if *a* is greater than or equal to 1 or *b* is greater than or equal to 1, then go to move."

The reader is encouraged to satisfy himself that these three statements accomplish exactly the same thing.

It should be noted carefully that in the construction **if** . . . **then** . . . **else** the **else** is sometimes optional and sometimes required. We may state the rule as follows: in an if-statement, that is, a statement beginning with the word **if,** the **else** is optional; in a conditional expression appearing within an arithmetic expression or a go to statement the **else** is required. Thus we are allowed to write either of the following forms:

if a = 6 **then** y := 2;

if b = 0 **then** z := 0 **else** q := 9;

However, it is *not* permissible to write

g := **if** c = 1 **then** x ↑ 2;

because there is nothing to specify what should be done in case *c* is not equal to 1.

Further examples of Boolean expressions appear in Case Study 2, Section 3.8.

3.7 Case Study 1: Column Design

A mechanical engineer wishes to obtain data for plotting a curve of the safe loading of a certain type of column as a function of the slimness ratio of the column. He has selected from a handbook two empirical formulas that give the safe loading in two ranges of the slimness ratio.

$$S = \begin{cases} 17{,}000 - 0.485\,R^2 & \text{for} \quad R < 120 \\[2mm] \dfrac{18{,}000}{1 + \dfrac{R^2}{18{,}000}} & \text{for} \quad R \geq 120 \end{cases}$$

where
S = safe load, pounds/in.^{2}
R = slimness ratio

The safe loading is to be calculated for slimness ratios of 20 to 200 in steps of 5. This range of values can be expressed in the convenient notation (mathematical notation, not ALGOL):

$$\text{slimness ratio} = 20(5)200$$

This is not a very difficult task. We need to set up the iteration on R, which requires setting $R = 20$ before getting into the body of the computation, together with some sort of testing and incrementing scheme. Suppose we arrange the latter as follows: after each time through the "loop" we will ask whether the value of R just used was less than 200; if it was, we still have more values of R to use, so we add 5 to R and go around the loop again. On the other hand, if the value of R just used was 200 or greater, we are done.

The main computation is a simple matter of determining from the value of R the formula that applies and computing S accordingly. A block diagram of the procedure is shown in Figure 3.5.

In writing the ALGOL program, there is only one area in which the way to go about it is not perfectly obvious and that is in writing the statements to handle the two different formulas. Shall we write

if $R < 120$ **then** ...   or   **if** $R \geq 120$ **then** ...?

This makes no difference at all, as long as the appropriate assignment statement is associated with whatever way we choose. In the same connection, what is the best way to go about the selection of one of the two formulas? One way would be with an if-statement without the **else:**

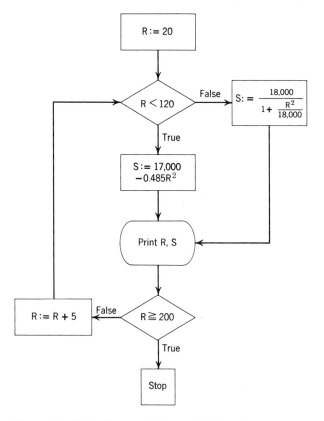

Figure 3.5. Block diagram of the method of solution of Case Study 1.

if $R < 120$ **then begin**

$S := 17000 - 0.485 \times R \times R$;

go to around **end**;

$S := 18000/(1 + R \times R/18000)$;

around:

This is a bit awkward because of the necessity of skipping around the second formula after executing the first. If we were going to do it this way at all, a single if-then-else statement would be better:

if $R < 120$ **then** $S := 17000 - 0.485 \times R \uparrow 2$ **else**

$S := 18000/(1 + R \uparrow 2/18000)$;

(It is largely immaterial whether we write $R \uparrow 2$ or $R \times R$.)

A better approach, because it is neater and simpler (and likely to be faster for the object program), is to take advantage of the ability to put an if-clause in an assignment statement. This is probably the best approach whenever a single vari-

```
        begin real R, S;
        R := 20;
again:  S := if R < 120 then 17000 − 0.485 × R ↑ 2 else 18000/(1 + R ↑ 2/18000),
        Print (R, S);
        if R ≧ 200 then Stop;
        R := R + 5;
        go to again
        end
```

Figure 3.6. ALGOL program for Case Study 1.

able is to be set equal to one of several expressions.

$$S := \text{if } R < 120 \text{ then } 17000 - 0.485 \times R \uparrow 2 \text{ else}$$

$$18000/(1 + R \uparrow 2/18000);$$

The complete program is shown in Figure 3.6.

3.8   Case Study 2: A Logical Problem in Surveying

A surveyor has been given data on a great many quadrilaterals. He would like to make a preliminary analysis of the areas represented by the data, to determine for each whether it is

a square;
a rectangle (but not a square);
a rhombus (but not a square or rectangle);
a parallelogram (but not a square, rectangle, or rhombus);
none of these.

Let us label the diagram as shown in Figure 3.7. How can we go about determining the shape of the figure, given only the four sides and the four angles?

A necessary and sufficient condition for a quadrilateral to be a square or a rectangle is that all

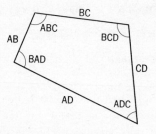

Figure 3.7. Naming of the four sides and four angles of the quadrilateral of Case Study 2.

four angles be 90°. A tentative starting point in the analysis would be a statement of the general form

$$\text{if } ABC = 90 \text{ then } \ldots$$

This will not do, however: physical measurements are not exact. We will be willing to accept the figure as a rectangle or square if the angles are all within some small tolerance of 90°. Suppose we leave the size of this tolerance to the discretion of the surveyor; in other words, one of the inputs to the program will be a number named, say, *angtoler*. The program must be set up so that an angle *on either side* of 90° by no more than this tolerance will be accepted. The easiest way to do this is with a relation of the type

$$\text{abs } (ABC - 90) < angtoler$$

There are four angles to be tested; we are interested in knowing whether *all* of them will meet the test. The simple way to do this is with an if-clause having four such relations combined with logical *ands*.

It is clearly going to be necessary to test some combinations of sides for near-equality also. Here, we had better set up the tolerance in terms of a *relative* error, since we have no information about the dimensions of the areas: an error of a foot might be acceptable in a large area but not close enough in a small one. This kind of test can be set up in several different ways. One that seems reasonable is to accept the two sides as "equal" if the difference between their lengths is less than a prescribed tolerance multiplied by the sum of their lengths. If we call this tolerance *sidetoler*, the test will be of the general form

$$\text{if abs } (AB - CD) < sidetoler$$

$$\times (AB + CD) \text{ then } \ldots$$

Now let us see if we can devise a sequence of tests that will establish the shape of the figure. This, too, can be done in many ways. Here is one:

The figure is a square if all angles are 90° and any two adjacent sides, say AB and BC, are equal.

If it is not a square, it is a rectangle if all angles are 90°.

If it is neither a square nor a rectangle, it is a rhombus if all sides are the same. This test can be made by asking whether $AB = BC$, $AB = CD$, and $AB = AD$; if each of the other three is equal to AB, all are the same.

If it is none of the above, it is still a parallelogram if both pairs of opposite sides are equal, that is, if $AB = CD$ and $BC = AD$.

It is important that the tests be made in this order, since we want to print out the most restrictive definition that the figure satisfies. All of the others are special cases of the parallelogram, but we want to call a square a square, not a parallelogram. The only exception is that since a rectangle and a rhombus are not special cases of each other the order of the two tests is arbitrary.

So far we have established the basic decision logic. Now we must investigate the simplest way to state the algorithm in ALGOL. It would be possible, of course, to write out long if-statements expressing each of the rules above, but doing so would result in an unnecessarily long program since we would be making the same tests repeatedly. It appears that it would be helpful if there were some way to set up a variable that would be true if a test were satisfied and false if it were not. And there is: this is precisely what a Boolean variable permits. We can conveniently take advantage of three Boolean variables here, which we call *angles*, *oppsides*, and *adjsides*, defined as follows:

angles is true if all angles are within the tolerance of 90°

oppsides is true if $AB = CD$, within the tolerance
adjsides is true if $AB = BC$, within the tolerance

Each of the Boolean variables will be used at least twice. In addition, we will have to test two other pairs of sides for equality, once each, but there is not much point in setting up Boolean variables for them; nothing would be saved since they are used only once.

With these Boolean variables it is quite simple to make the tests that establish what figure we have. The test for a square, for instance, is just

$$\text{angles} \land \text{adjsides}$$

Recall that *angles* is true if and only if all angles are 90°; *adjsides* is true if and only if the two adjacent sides are equal. The Boolean expression *angles* $\land$ *adjsides* is true if and only if both variables are true. Recall finally that an if-clause permits any Boolean expression; the relations that we have used in all examples so far are merely special cases of Boolean expressions.

```
begin real AB, BC, CD, AD, ABC, BCD, ADC, BAD, angtoler, sidetoler;
      boolean angles, oppsides, adjsides; integer case;
Read (angtoler, sidetoler);
Nextcase: Read (case, AB, BC, CD, AD, ABC, BCD, ADC, BAD);
angles := abs (ABC − 90) < angtoler ∧ abs (BCD − 90) < angtoler
          ∧ abs (ADC − 90) < angtoler ∧ abs (BAD − 90) < angtoler;
oppsides := abs (AB − CD) < sidetoler × (AB + CD);
adjsides := abs (AB − BC) < sidetoler × (AB + BC);
if angles ∧ adjsides then begin Print ('square'); go to Nextcase end;
if angles then begin Print ('rectangle'); go to Nextcase end;
if oppsides ∧ adjsides ∧ abs (AB − AD) < sidetoler × (AB + AD) then
      begin Print ('rhombus'); go to Nextcase end;
if oppsides ∧ abs (BC − AD) < sidetoler × (BC + AD) then
      begin Print ('parallelogram'); go to Nextcase end;
Print ('none');
go to Nextcase
end
```

Figure 3.8. Program to determine the shape of a quadrilateral, given sides and angles.

```
ANGTOLER    1.0000    SIDETOLER    .0100
```

CASE	AB	BC	CD	AD	ABC	BCD	ADC	BAD	FIGURE
1	50.00	50.00	50.00	50.00	90.00	90.00	90.00	90.00	SQUARE
2	50.10	49.70	50.00	50.20	90.00	90.80	89.10	89.50	SQUARE
3	50.10	49.10	52.00	53.50	90.00	91.20	88.70	90.20	NONE
4	22.30	87.10	22.40	87.00	90.00	90.10	90.20	89.90	RECTANGLE
5	63.00	63.10	63.20	62.80	41.60	138.40	41.50	138.50	RHOMBUS
6	130.00	264.00	131.00	263.00	23.40	156.60	23.40	156.10	PARALLELOGRAM
7	141.40	100.00	141.40	300.00	135.00	135.00	45.00	45.00	NONE
8	100.00	200.00	300.00	400.00	1.00	2.00	3.00	900.00	NONE
9	200.00	200.00	800.00	9999.00	90.00	90.00	90.00	90.00	SQUARE
10	100.00	100.00	100.00	100.00	60.00	60.00	60.00	.00	RHOMBUS
11	100.00	200.00	100.00	200.00	60.00	300.00	300.00	60.00	PARALLELOGRAM

Figure 3.9

The program can now be written. The declaration must list *angles, oppsides,* and *adjsides* as Boolean so that the ALGOL processor will set them up as having only logical values. The declaration will list a variable named *case* as being the integer type; this is simply a case number to be read in with the data for each figure to make identification of the output easier.

In reading the program of Figure 3.8, remember that an assignment statement for a Boolean variable must have a Boolean expression on the right and that a simple relation is a Boolean expression. If the value of the expression is true, the variable is given the logical value true; if the expression is false, the variable is given the value false. Note the Print operations here, which contain words to be printed on the report rather than the names of variables. When a string of letters and/or digits is not to be regarded as a variable identifier but as a thing in itself, it is enclosed in *string quotes;* the string is then sometimes called a *literal.* The output procedure must naturally be able to accept literals, which we assume for our hypothetical input and output procedures.

This program was run on a computer with several sets of data after modifying the Print statements to include the sides and angles in the output. Headings were also printed. The results are shown in Figure 3.9. Exercise 9 asks you to correct the program to avoid the nonsense in cases 9, 10, and 11.

EXERCISES

1. Write statements to do the following.

* a. If a is greater than b, set x equal to 16.9, but if a is less than or equal to b set y equal to 23.1.

b. If rho + theta $< 10^{-6}$, transfer to the statement labeled *alldone;* otherwise do nothing.

* c. If rho + theta $< 10^{-6}$, transfer to the statement labeled *alldone;* otherwise transfer to the statement labeled *oncemore.*

d. If sigma > 6, set *sw1* equal to 1; otherwise set *sw2* equal to 1.

* e. If g and h are both negative, set *signs* $= -1$; if both are positive, set *signs* $= +1$; if they have different signs, set *signs* $= 0$. (Note that it is permissible to use an identifier like "signs." The addition of the s makes it essentially different from the function identifier "sign.")

* f. If $0.999 < x < 1.001$, transfer to *wrapup;* otherwise transfer to *start new iteration.*

g. If $a < 0$ and $b > 0$, or if $c = 0$, set *lambda* equal to $\cos(x + 1.2)$; otherwise do nothing.

* h. If $i = 1$ and $R < S$, transfer to statement 261; if $i = 1$ and $R \geqq S$, transfer to statement 257; if $i \neq 1$, transfer to statement 297.

i. If $N = 1, 2,$ or 8, transfer to statement 250; if $N = 3$ or 7, transfer to statement 251; if $N = 4, 5,$ or 6, transfer to statement 252; if N is none of these, transfer to statement 9999.

* j. At a certain point in a program it is necessary to transfer to

(1) the statement labeled *first*   if $i = 1$
(2) the statement labeled *between*   if $1 < i < N$
(3) the statement labeled *last*   if $i = N$

* k. Place whichever of the variables X and Y is algebraically larger in Big. If $X = Y$, place either of them in Big.

l. Place whichever of the variables X and Y is larger in absolute value in Bigabs.

* m. Xreal and Ximag are the real and imaginary parts of a complex number. Transfer to *square* if Xreal and Ximag are both less than 1 in absolute value.

n. Transfer to *circle* if $\sqrt{\text{Xreal}^2 + \text{Ximag}^2} < 1$.

o. Transfer to *diamond* if the point with the coordinates Xreal and Ximag lies within a square of side $\sqrt{2}$ with its corners on the coordinate axes.

2. Write statements, or groups of statements, to do the following.

* a. Compute

$$P = \begin{cases} \dfrac{\pi}{2} e^{-m} & \text{if } m > 0 \\ 0 & \text{if } m = 0 \\ \dfrac{\pi}{2} e^{+m} & \text{if } m < 0 \end{cases}$$

b. Compute

$$Q = a1, \qquad x < b1$$
$$= a2, \ b1 \leqq x < b2$$
$$= a3, \ b2 \leqq x < b3$$
$$= a4, \ b3 \leqq x$$

* c. Set

$$\text{switchg} = 1 \quad \text{if } k < 0$$
$$= 2 \quad \text{if } k = 0$$
$$= 3 \quad \text{if } k > 0$$

d. Set *line* = 1 if

$$N1 + 2 = N2 + 1 = N3$$
$$\text{or if } N1 + 4 = N2 + 2 = N3$$
$$\text{or if } N1 + 6 = N2 + 3 = N3$$
$$\text{or if } N1 + 8 = N2 + 4 = N3$$

Set *line* = 0 otherwise.

e. If $Y1 < Y2 > Y3$, go to *local max*, and to *again* if not.

f. Compute

$$y = \begin{cases} a + bx + cx^2 & \text{if } k = 1 \\ d + ex + fx^2 & \text{if } k = 2 \\ g + hx + ix^2 & \text{if } k = 3 \end{cases}$$

Note. In the remaining exercises you are asked to write complete program blocks, including declarations. All variables may be taken to be of type real, except in Exercise 9.

*3. *Y* is to be computed as a function of *x* according to

$$y = 16.7x + 9.2x^2 - 1.02x^3$$

for *x* values from 1.0 to 9.9, inclusive, in steps of 0.1. Write a program segment to print *x* and *y* for each of the 90 values of *x*.

4. *Y* is to be computed as a function of *x* according to

$$y = \frac{a + b \cos x}{ax^2 - bx^3 \sin x}$$

for *x* values from 0.5 to 8.5 in steps of 0.05. Write a program segment to print *x* and *y* for each of the 161 values of *x*, except that if the denominator is less than 10^{-3} in absolute value set *y* equal to 10^7 instead of evaluating the formula.

*5. Write a program segment to carry out the processing required in Exercise 8 of Chapter 1.

6. Write a program segment to carry out the processing required in Exercise 9 of Chapter 1.

*7. Write a program segment to carry out the processing required in Exercise 10 of Chapter 1.

8. Write a single assignment statement to carry out the processing required in Exercise 11 of Chapter 1.

9. The results printed in Figure 3.9 show the analysis of the possibilities to be somewhat lacking in that a lot depends on receiving sensible data. Add tests to the program of Figure 3.8 to make the identification ironclad. *Hint.* Consider whether it would suffice to test that the supposed quadrilateral actually has four nonzero sides and that it is closed (or nearly so).

*10. Given *a*, *b*, and *n*, and

$$f(x) = \frac{\sqrt{x} \sin x}{x + e^x}$$

compute

$$\text{Trapezoidal} = \frac{h}{2} [f(a) + 2f(a + h) + 2f(a + 2h) + \cdots$$
$$+ 2f(b - 2h) + 2f(b - h) + f(b)$$

where

$$n = \frac{b - a}{n}$$

11. Same as Exercise 10, except compute

$$\text{Simpsons} = \frac{h}{3} [f(a) + 4f(a + h) + 2f(a + 2h)$$
$$+ 4f(a + 3h) + \cdots + 4f(b - 3h)$$
$$+ 2f(b - 2h) + 4f(b - h) + f(b)]$$

where *n* is now assumed to be even.

4. THE for-STATEMENT

4.1 Introduction

One of the most frequent operations in computing is the repetition of some calculation, each time with a different value of what is called the *controlled variable*. We saw an elementary example of such a computation in Case Study 1, in which the safe loading of a column was found for many values of a slimness ratio. As we proceed, we shall see that there are many other situations in which something of this general character must be done. It is quite valuable, therefore, to have language features that simplify these operations. The ALGOL *for-statement* provides wide flexibility in this respect.

The general form of the ALGOL for-statement is

for variable : = for–list **do** statement

The for-list is composed of one or more *for-list elements,* which may be of several types. The simplest for-list element is an arithmetic expression (which includes single variables and single numbers, remember). The basic idea of the for-statement is that the statement following the **do** is executed repeatedly, with the controlled variable taking on the successive values specified by the for-list. If several statements are to be repeated under control of a for-statement, they must be made into a compound statement by enclosing them between **begin** and **end.**

As an elementary example, suppose that it is necessary to compute and print the value of the expression

$$y = \frac{x^3}{3} - \frac{a^3}{3} \log|a^3 + x^3|$$

for $x = -2.0, -1.2, 1.7, 2.4,$ and $4.9.$ This is as easily done as said, as shown in Figure 4.1. This compound statement will be executed five times, with x taking on the successive values given in the for-list.

A much more powerful form of for-list element is the step-until type, in which we are able to specify an initial value for the controlled variable, an increment, and a final value. A complete for-statement having this type of for-list has the general form

for variable : = initial **step** increment
until final **do** statement;

"Initial," "increment," and "final" can be any arithmetic expressions. Execution of this statement proceeds as follows. The controlled variable is first set equal to the value of the "initial" expression. If the value of the controlled variable is not greater than the value of the "final" expression, the statement following the **do** is executed;

```
for x : = −2.0, −1.2, 1.7, 2.4, 4.9 do
     begin
     y : = (x ↑ 3 − a ↑ 3
        × ln (abs (a ↑ 3 + x ↑ 3)))/3;
     Print (x, y)
     end
```

Figure 4.1. An elementary example of a for-statement.

36

```
begin real R, S;
for R : = 20 step 5 until 200 do
    begin
    S : = if R < 120 then 17000 − 0.485 × R ↑ 2 else 18000/(1 + R ↑ 2/18000);
    Print (R, S)
    end
end
```

Figure 4.2. Program for Case Study 1, using the for-statement.

otherwise, control passes to the statement following the complete for-statement. After executing the statement following the **do,** the controlled variable is increased by the value of the "increment" expression and the test for completion is made again.

We can begin to illustrate the power of this heavily used statement by rewriting the program for Case Study 1 that was shown on page 32. Figure 4.2 shows how much simpler the program becomes with the for-step-until construction.

Note in the explanation of the for-step-until construction that the statement following the **do** is executed until the value of the controlled variable *exceeds* the value of the "final" expression. That is, if the "initial" and "increment" expressions lead to a value of the controlled variable equal to the "final" value, then the statement following the **do** *will* be executed for that value. In the program of Figure 4.2, for instance, the formula *is* evaluated for $x = 200$.

Actually, the description above is not quite precise in referring to an *increment* and in the reference to *exceeding* the value of the "final" expression. The "increment" can, in fact, be negative, in which case the test for continuation is to determine whether the value of the controlled variable is *less* than the value of the "final" expression. For instance, if it were desired to compute the safe loading for slimness ratios starting with 200 and working down to 20, the for-statement in Figure 4.2 could be written

for R : = 200 **step** −5 **until** 20 **do**

The operation of this type of for-statement can be expressed in terms of a group of ALGOL statements in a way that is entirely equivalent and which displays the complete logic of the operation a little more clearly. For conciseness, write the statement in the form

for V : = A **step** B **until** C **do** S_1; S_2

The result of this statement is the same as the result of statements:

```
        V : = A;
L:      if (V − C) × sign (B) > 0 then go to S₂;
        Statement S₁;
        V : = V + B;
        go to L;
```

It is quite important to realize that "sign (B)" means the sign of the *value* of B, not whether the expression B as written begins with a minus sign. For instance, this group of two statements will *decrease* the value of the controlled variable X:

```
        N : = −7;
        for X : = 90 step N until 4 do
```

In most situations this kind of consideration does not arise, but it is occasionally necessary to refer back to the precise definition contained in the set of equivalent statements above. Bearing in mind that A, B, and C in that definition can be complete arithmetic expressions and that the sign of the expressions may change during the repeated execution of the statements controlled by the for-statement, this analysis can become quite complex. Situations of such complexity are uncommon.

The controlled statement of a for-statement must never be entered except by executing the for-statement; that is, a go to leading into the controlled statement from outside it is illegal. (Note the phrase *from outside it;* this does not prohibit a compound controlled statement that contains go to statements.)

A compound controlled statement *is* allowed to have a go to that leads completely outside the controlled statement. If this is done, the repetition stops, of course, regardless of the status of the termination conditions in the for-statement.

The step-until for-list allows great flexibility in the specification of the starting and incrementing expressions but somewhat less freedom in the method of stopping the repetition. The third type of for-list, that based on the *while* construction, takes away some of the flexibility in starting and incrementing but provides almost complete freedom in the method of stopping.

The general form of a for-statement based on this for-list element is

$$\textbf{for } V := E \textbf{ while } F \textbf{ do } S_1; S_2$$

E is any arithmetic expression and *F* is any Boolean expression. Every repetition of the execution of such a construction is exactly the same: *V*, the controlled variable, is set equal to *E*; if the Boolean expression is still true, statement S_1 is executed and the process repeated; if the Boolean expression is not true, statement S_2 is executed, stopping the repetition. The operation can be more concisely described by the following equivalent program:

$$
\begin{aligned}
&L: \qquad V := E; \\
&\qquad\quad \textbf{if } \neg F \textbf{ then go to } S_2; \\
&\qquad\quad \text{Statement } S_1; \\
&\qquad\quad \textbf{go to } L;
\end{aligned}
$$

It is important to notice that the controlled variable is set equal to the arithmetic expressions each time the controlled statement is repeated. This means in practice that the controlled variable must be given a starting value before entering the for-statement; the for-statement then handles only the modification of the controlled variable and the testing. This initialization of the controlled variable can also be handled (and somewhat more smoothly) by using a for-statement of the form

$$\textbf{for } V := E_1, E_2 \textbf{ while } B \textbf{ do}$$

That is, the initialization can be done within the for-statement itself.

A simple example of the operation of this type of statement is provided by rewriting the program of Case Study 1 with a for-while construction. All that need be done is to replace the for-statement in Figure 4.2 with the statement

$$\textbf{for } R := 15, R + 5 \textbf{ while } R \leq 200 \textbf{ do}$$

This example shows only how it is possible to carry out the calculation with either the for-step-until method or the for-while method; it does not demonstrate the power of the for-while technique. For an illustration of the simplification made possible by the latter, consider a standard method of computing a square root. To find the square root *x*, of a number *A*, we repeatedly apply the formula

$$x = \frac{1}{2}\left(\frac{A}{\text{prevx}} + \text{prevx}\right)$$

The number *prevx* is initially given some starting value, from which we calculate an approximation to the root, *x*. If *x* and *prevx* are sufficiently close together, then *x* is the square root and we stop the process; if the two are not close, then *prevx* is given the value *x* and the process is repeated. The basis of this technique, which is known as the Newton-Raphson method, is given in calculus courses but can be explained quite easily without calculus. Suppose first that *prevx* is in fact the square root of *A*. Then we have

$$
\begin{aligned}
x &= \frac{1}{2}\left(\frac{A}{\text{prevx}} + \text{prevx}\right) \\
&= \frac{1}{2}\left(\frac{A}{\sqrt{A}} + \sqrt{A}\right) \\
&= \frac{1}{2}(\sqrt{A} + \sqrt{A}) = \sqrt{A}
\end{aligned}
$$

Suppose next that *prevx* is less than the square root of *x*. Then *A* divided by something *less* than its square root gives a quotient *greater* than its square root; we are thus repeatedly taking the average of two numbers, one greater and one less than the square root. A similar analysis applies if *prevx* is greater than the square root of *A*.

A program to carry out this repetitive calculation involves four operations: obtaining a starting value for *prevx*, carrying out the evaluation of the formula, testing for completion, and assigning the newly computed value of *x* to *prevx* if the process is not completed. These operations can be built into a for-while construction in several ways, of which we shall show one.

The first step in this program is to set *prevx* equal to a starting value before going into the for-statement. The starting value has a significant influence on the number of *iterations* (repetitions) of the process that will be required to converge to the square root, but in fact the process will converge for any positive starting value; in this program we shall start with 1 and not worry about the number of iterations that may be required. The for-statement will be used to calculate a new value of *x* and then to test whether the absolute value of the difference between *x* and *prevx* is less than some preassigned tolerance. If they are the same or nearly the same, the operation of the for-while construction will stop the iteration; if they are not the same, we will execute a simple assignment statement that gives *prevx* the value of *x* and repeat the calculation and testing. The program is shown in Figure 4.3.

prevx : = 1;
for x : = 0.5 × (A/prevx + prevx) **while** abs (x − prevx) $>_{10}-6$ **do** prevx : = x;

The tolerance, it may be seen, has been arbitrarily chosen as 10^{-6}. Note the absolute value function: although it happens that convergence is always from above, the first time the test is made in computing the root of a number less than 1 the difference will be negative. Without the absolute value, the loop would stop before it ever really got started.

This method, or some variation of it, is almost always used to calculate square roots in digital computers. With ALGOL, we do not have to write out this little procedure; the same general approach is called into action when we write *sqrt*. Since this kind of program tends to be employed frequently, great effort is put into making it as fast as possible. In particular, various schemes are used to get a starting value that is at least a fair approximation to the square root in order to reduce the number of iterations required. In fact, if the starting value is good enough, it is sometimes possible to repeat the calculation a fixed number of times without any testing.

This example brings up a feature of all versions of the for-statement that must be kept constantly in mind: upon exit from the for-statement by exhaustion of the for-list, the value of the controlled variable is undefined. In this example the result is that one cannot assume that *x* will in fact have the value of the square root when the computation has been completed. Here the restriction is of little importance, for, when repetition stops, *x* and *prevx* must have nearly the same value anyway, and we can call *prevx* the square root.

Note that this restriction does not apply to a variable that is set equal to the controlled variable within the for-statement, as in this example. From this one could guess that the reason for the restriction is that the testing for completion can cause the controlled variable to be changed, at least in some processors.

Note, finally, that if the repetition is terminated by encountering a go to statement within the loop the value of the controlled variable *is* defined; the restriction applies only after completion of the loop by exhaustion of the for-list.

The off-hand choice of 10^{-6} as the tolerance for stopping the repetition is worth a short digression with much broader application than this example.

We encounter no difficulty here as long as the number of which we want the square root is somewhere in the vicinity of 1 to 100; but what happens if it is very large or very small? As it happens, we get into very serious difficulties either way. Suppose, first, that we are trying to take the square root of 10^{-30}. The program is set up to stop repeating as soon as two approximations are the same within 10^{-6}; this will happen long before the correct square root of 10^{-15} is reached. As a matter of fact, the "square root" would be given as about $9.5 \cdot 10^{-7}$. Thus we see that the procedure stops too soon in this case.

For a very large number, on the other hand, it may *never* stop! Suppose we try to take the square root of $2 \cdot 10^{20}$. To express the answer to six decimal places requires 16 digits, but most computers carry ALGOL real variables to only eight or ten places (plus the exponent that locates the decimal point). Thus it will be only by chance that two approximations can ever agree to the required accuracy, and the while construction will never get us out of the computation.

It is well to keep this kind of consideration in mind in any work with a computer. In this particular case we got into trouble by specifying an *absolute* accuracy, and we can get out of it by changing to *relative* accuracy. In other words, instead of asking that two approximations be the same to within a tolerance, we could ask that their difference be less than some small fraction of one of them, say the most recent. The for-statement would then be

for x : = 0.5 × (A/prevx + prevx)
    while abs (x − prevx) $>_{10}-6$ × x **do**

In other situations in which the precision is a problem other remedies may be necesary.

This introduction may be completed with a formal definition of the for-statement, in which we give precise definitions of some terms used above.

A *for-list element* may be any of the following:

1. arithmetic expression
2. arithmetic expression **step** arithmetic expression **until** arithmetic expression
3. arithmetic expression **while** Boolean expression

```
begin real v3v2, firstR, incR, lastR, firstgamma, incgamma,
    lastgamma, R, gamma, Eff;
Read (v3v2, firstR, incR, lastR, firstgamma, incgamma, lastgamma);
for R : = firstR step incR until lastR do
for gamma : = firstgamma step incgamma until lastgamma do
    begin
    Eff : = 1 − 1/R ↑ (gamma − 1) × (v3v2 ↑ gamma − 1)/(gamma × (v3v2 − 1));
    Print (v3v2, R, gamma, Eff)
    end
end
```

Figure 4.4. Diesel efficiency program.

A *for-list* is any one or more of these, separated by commas if there is more than one.

A *for-clause* has the general form

for variable : = for-list **do**

A for-statement consists of a for-clause followed by any statement, possibly compound; the for-statement may have a label.

The main thing that these definitions tell us is that a for-statement may have any number of for-list elements, possibly of different types.

The following are acceptable for-statements:

for N : = 1, 2, 6 **step** 2 **until** 14, 17, 26 **do**
    Statement;
    (*N* would take on the successive values 1, 2, 6, 8, 10, 12, 14, 17, and 26.)
for G : = rho ↑ 2 **step** sigma/6 **until** final **do**
    Statement;
for theta : = −61.8 **step** −x ↑ 2 **until** −90, −96 **do**
    Statement;
for a : = 2, 4, 6, a + 3 **while** y > epsilon **do**
    Statement;
for beta : = 23.08, 26 **step** 1 **until** gamma + 2,
    beta ↑ 2 **while** sqrt (a ↑ 2 + b ↑ 2) > toler,
    2.958 **do**
    Statement;

4.2 Further Examples of the Use of the for-Statement

Two examples bring out additional ways of employing the for-statement and at the same time are rather typical of small problems that can be solved easily with ALGOL.

We have emphasized that the statement following the **do** may be any statement and that it is often compound. In particular, it can be another

for-statement, and the compound statement can contain a **for**.

Consider the following problem. One form of the equation for the theoretical efficiency of a Diesel engine is

$$\text{Efficiency} = 1 - \frac{1}{R^{\gamma-1}} \left[\frac{\left(\dfrac{v_3}{v_2}\right)^{\gamma} - 1}{\gamma\left(\dfrac{v_3}{v_2} - 1\right)} \right]$$

where R = compression ratio
    γ = ratio of specific heats
    $\dfrac{v_3}{v_2}$ = load ratio

An engineer wishes to study the variation of efficiency with changes in R and γ for a fixed value of v_3/v_2. He wishes to be able to run the program several times, perhaps using a different fixed v_3/v_2 and perhaps with different ranges of values of R and γ.

It seems reasonable to set up the program so that it will read in a value of v_3/v_2 along with enough data to specify the ranges of R and γ. Each range can be specified by reading in a starting value, an increment, and a final value. The formation of all combinations of values of R and γ can readily be accomplished with two "nested" for-statements.

A program is shown in Figure 4.4, most of which is self-explanatory. The names chosen for the variables are obvious, but it is worth noting that v_3/v_2 could not be used. (Why?) The two for-statements operate as follows. The first one sets a value of R, then the second one runs through all values of γ. When the second for-statement has been completed, the first one steps the value of R and the second one again runs through all values of γ, etc. Thus we get all combinations with a minimum of effort.

This program illustrates a matter of definition that is quite important in understanding ALGOL: Statement parentheses **begin-end** are *not* needed around the second for-statement. What follows the **do** in the first for-statement must be a single statement, and it is: the second for-statement. The fact that the "single" statement is itself compound and contains several other statements is immaterial.

For a second example, consider a problem in plotting the frequency response of a certain servomechanism. The response is given by

$$T\,(i\omega) = \frac{K}{i\omega(1 + iT_1\omega)(1 + iT_2\omega)}$$

where ω = angular frequency, radians per second
$\quad\;\; i = \sqrt{-1}$
$\quad\; T$ = transfer function
T_1, T_2 = time constants, seconds

An electrical engineer wishes to be able to read in values of K, T_1, and T_2 and compute the transfer function for a number of values of ω. The transfer function will, in general, be a complex number. The simplest way to handle the complex arithmetic in this case is to rewrite the formula so that the real and imaginary parts are separated. All arithmetic will then involve only real quantities—which is all we can deal with in any case. By rewriting the formula in the simplest form, we get

$$T\,(i\omega) = \frac{-K\,(T_1 + T_2)}{(1 + T_1{}^2\omega^2)(1 + T_2{}^2\omega^2)}$$
$$- \frac{K(1 - T_1T_2\omega^2)}{\omega(1 + T_1{}^2\omega^2)(1 + T_2{}^2\omega^2)} \cdot i$$

The real and imaginary parts of T are to be printed for each of a range of values of ω. We will read in a starting and final value of ω, as we have done before, but this time the manner of increasing ω will be a little more flexible. A number C and a number L will be read. If L is zero, C is to be *added* to ω between repetitions, but if L is not zero ω is to be *multiplied* by C. In either case the computation is to be continued until T has been computed with the largest value of ω not exceeding the specified final value of ω.

The decision whether to add or to multiply by C can be handled in many ways. Here we put the choice in the for-statement, mostly to illustrate what can be done. The automatic modification of the controlled variable in a for-statement always *adds* the value of the step expression to the variable; there is no way to change the execution of the for-statement to make it multiply. However, what is added can be the value of *any* arithmetic expression. Observe, then, that $C\omega = \omega + C\omega - \omega$. If L is nonzero, therefore, specifying multiplication, we will add $C\omega - \omega$ to ω.

We must still find a way to make the choice between the two methods of changing ω. This could, of course, be done with an if-statement and two for-statements, but it can be done much more neatly by taking advantage of the fact that the step expression may include an if-clause.

The program shown in Figure 4.5 is not especially complicated. Note that an intermediate variable named D has been set up to avoid two computations of a factor that is common to the denominators of both formulas. This practice is recommended.

It is unfortunately not true that the most elegant source program is always the most efficient on the computer. In this program it is a bit awkward to have to make the decision whether to add or multi-

```
begin real K, T1, T2, omegastart, omegalast, C, L, omega, D, Treal, Timag;
Read (K, T1, T2, omegastart, omegalast, C, L);
for omega : = omegastart step if L = 0 then C else C × omega − omega until omegalast do
    begin
    D : = (1 + (T1 × omega) ↑ 2) × (1 + (T2 × omega) ↑ 2);
    Treal : = −K × (T1 + T2)/D;
    Timag : = −K × (1 − T1 × T2 × omega ↑ 2)/(omega × D);
    Print (K, T1, T2, omega, Treal, Timag)
    end
end
```

Figure 4.5. Servomechanism frequency response program.

ply every time the formula is evaluated, when it could be settled at the outset. In a small program like this one it would not matter much in running time of the object program. In larger programs things like this can make a big difference. The following case study makes this point rather graphically.

4.3 Case Study 3: Heat Transfer

A heat transfer problem has been formulated to require evaluation of the series

$$T(\rho, \theta) = \frac{800}{\pi^2} \left[\left(\frac{\rho}{10}\right) \sin \theta - \frac{1}{3^2} \left(\frac{\rho}{10}\right)^3 \sin 3\theta \right.$$
$$\left. + \frac{1}{5^2} \left(\frac{\rho}{10}\right)^5 \sin 5\theta - + \cdots \right]$$

The ranges of interest are $0 \le \rho \le 10$ and $0 \le \theta \le \pi$; in these ranges convergence is assured. All we need to do is to determine how many terms are required for sufficient accuracy.

The analysis of the error committed by truncating the series after a finite number of terms poses some difficulties. Although the series is absolutely convergent (that is, it would converge even if all the signs were plus), it is only "approximately" alternating because of the minus sign that is introduced by the sine function. Therefore, we cannot say that the error committed is less than the first term neglected, as we could if the terms alternated in sign. For the moment, let us take a conservative (and perhaps careless) approach and use 40 terms of the series, regardless of the size of

ρ and θ. This is probably a great deal more than adequate, but we will not worry now about the possible waste of computer time.

We may exhibit this formula in a way that makes it a little more obvious how a for-loop can be set up to evaluate it.

$$T(\rho, \theta) = \frac{800}{\pi^2} \sum_{i=1}^{40} \frac{(-1)^{i+1}}{(2i - 1)^2} \left(\frac{\rho}{10}\right)^{2i-1} \sin \left[(2i - 1) \, \theta\right]$$

The program in Figure 4.6 is simple enough to follow. The only thing that is not a straightforward counterpart of the formula is the mechanism for getting the power of -1. Raising -1 to a large power just to get an alternating sign would waste too much computer time; instead, we set up a variable that is $+1$ before going into the loop and reverse its sign after each execution.

Note the assignment statement in which *sum* is set equal to itself plus another term of the series. This is the customary way of forming a summation. The statement means to add the next term in the series to the present value of *sum* and to replace the value of *sum* with this new value. The technique works properly only if *sum* is made zero before going into the iteration, as we do just before the for-statement.

In practice, we would ordinarily compute the temperature at a network of points, using two for-loops to work through ranges of values of ρ and θ. However, we understand how this could be done and will not bother with the required statements. We simply read values of ρ and θ and compute the temperature at that particular point.

The programmer who sets up the evaluation of the formula this way is in for a rude shock. He

```
begin real rho, theta, i, signfactor, sum, Temp;
Read (rho, theta);
signfactor : = 1;
sum : = 0;
for i : = 1 step 1 until 40 do
        begin
        sum : = sum + signfactor/(2 × i − 1) ↑ 2 × (rho/10) ↑ (2 × i − 1) × sin ((2 × i − 1) × theta);
        signfactor : = −signfactor
        end;
Temp : = 800/9.8696 × sum;
Print (rho, theta, Temp)
end
```

Figure 4.6. Initial version of the heat transfer program.

```
begin real rho, theta, signfactor, sum, X, X2, angle, denom, test, Temp;
Read (rho, theta);
signfactor : = 1;
sum : = 0.0;
X : = rho/10.0;
X2 : = X × X;
angle : = theta;
denom : = 1.0;
for test : = X/denom ↑ 2 while test > ₁₀−4 do
    begin
    sum : = sum + signfactor × test × sin (angle);
    X : = X × X2;
    angle : = angle + 2 × theta;
    denom : = denom + 2.0;
    signfactor : = −signfactor
    end;
Temp : = 81.05696 × sum;
Print (rho, theta, Temp)
end
```

Figure 4.7. An improved version of the heat transfer program.

will discover when he runs the program that the speed of a computer can be completely wasted by careless problem analysis. The object program will be some five to ten times slower than necessary, the exact ratio depending on the size of ρ. If we bear in mind that this problem is much simpler than many that are solved on computers, it will be clear that some thought must be given to speed of execution of the object program.

A number of things can be done to improve the speed. To begin with, something must obviously be done to reduce the number of terms computed when a few will suffice. For instance, when $\rho = 1.0$, the third term of the series is less than 10^{-6}, regardless of the value of θ; it makes no sense to go on computing terms when a temperature accurate within 0.001 degree would be more than adequate for almost all applications. Even when $\rho = 9.0$, the twentieth term is less than 10^{-4}, regardless of the contribution of the sine function. We clearly need to set up a procedure for stopping the evaluation of the series after the terms have become smaller than some minimum value. This is not precisely correct, of course: in a test of the size of a term we must exclude the sine factor; otherwise we might incorrectly stop after finding a term that is small *only* because of the sine. We therefore set up the testing procedure so that it

will be carried out before multiplification by the sine.

A second likely candidate for time reduction is the raising of $\rho/10$ to a power. The method used in the program of Figure 4.6 is particularly bad, since the exponent is real (rather than an integer), and we recall from Section 2.3 that this is done in the object program by use of the formula

$$a \uparrow r = \exp (r \times \ln (a))$$

The computation of the exponential and the logarithm are both fairly time-consuming compared with arithmetic operations.

A much better technique is available in which $\rho/10$, which we will call X, and $(\rho/10)^2$, which we will call $X2$, are computed initially. Multiplying the two together gives $(\rho/10)^3$; multiplying this by $X2$ gives $(\rho/10)^5$, etc. This running computation of the next power of $(\rho/10)$ from the previous one is easily set up in the repeated statement of the for-loop.

Similarly, each new value of the angle in the sine function can be obtained by adding 2θ to the previous value of a variable that is initially set equal to θ. An equivalent process produces the $1/(2i - 1)^2$ factor.

If we rather arbitrarily establish the criterion that the evaluation of the series should be stopped as soon as the absolute value of a term (exclusive of the sine factor) becomes less than 10^{-4}, it will not be too difficult to set up the program with a for-while construction. We do have to be careful to get the system going properly, however. Before going into the for-loop, it will be necessary to establish the starting values of the various intermediate variables. Also, to avoid computing the test factor within the computation and in the for-loop testing, it would be a good idea to give this part of the term a name and use it in both places. This variable, which is called *test* in the program of Figure 4.7, must also be given some starting value; it must be larger than 10^{-4}, to avoid stopping the computation before it gets started. (Remember that testing in a for-statement is always done *before* executing the controlled statement.) The assignment of a value to this variable is done in the for-statement itself.

A careful study of Figures 4.6 and 4.7 will show that they do accomplish the same computation, although in rather different ways. Both programs have been run on a computer and do in fact give the same results.

The lessons of this case study are worth pondering. There is always more than one way to accomplish something, but the different ways are not always equally good.

4.4 Case Study 4: Luminous Efficiency

A black-body (perfect radiator) emits energy at a rate proportional to the fourth power of its temperature, according to the Stefan-Boltzmann equation

$$E = 36.9 \cdot 10^{-12} K^4$$

where E = emissive power, watts/cm^2
K = temperature, degrees Kelvin

We are interested in the fraction of this total energy contained in the visible spectrum, which is taken here to be $4 \cdot 10^{-5}$ to $7 \cdot 10^{-5}$ cm. We can get the visible part by integrating Planck's equation between these limits:

$$E_{visible} = \int_{4\cdot10^{-5}}^{7\cdot10^{-5}} \frac{2.39 \cdot 10^{-11} \, dx}{x^5 \left(e^{\frac{1.432}{Kx}} - 1\right)}$$

where x = wavelength, cm
E and K as before

The *luminous efficiency* is defined as the ratio of the energy in the visible spectrum to the total energy. If we multiply by 100 to get this efficiency in per cent and combine the constants, the problem will become that of evaluating

$$E_\% = \frac{64.77 \int_{4\cdot10^{-5}}^{7\cdot10^{-5}} \dfrac{dx}{x^5 \left(e^{\frac{1.432}{Kx}} - 1\right)}}{K^4}$$

The integral is evaluated by Simpson's rule, according to which

$$\int_a^b f(x) \, dx = \frac{h}{3} [f(a) + 4f(a+h) + 2f(a+2h)$$
$$+ 4f(a+3h) + \cdots + 2f(b-2h)$$
$$+ 4f(b-h) + f(b)]$$

where

$$h = \frac{b-a}{n}$$

and

n = number of intervals; n even

The summation of these terms can be carried out in several ways. The most efficient, from the standpoint of speed of the object program, is to accumulate the terms that are to be multiplied by 2 separately from those that are to be multiplied by 4. A minor difficulty is that there is one more term to be multiplied by 4 than to be multiplied by 2, which is an annoyance, since we would like to use one for-loop to accumulate both sums. This can be handled by using the for-loop to accumulate all but the last of the terms to be multiplied by 4, and then adding it in after getting out of the for-loop.

We can set up the for-loop to add $2h$ to the controlled variable x each time through, after starting with $a + h$. In this way x gives a term to be multiplied by 4, summed in sum4, and $x + h$ gives a term to be multiplied by 2, summed in sum2. After getting out of this loop, we can add in the terms for $x = a$, b, and $b - h$, multiply by $h/3$, and complete the calculation of the efficiency.

The program in Figure 4.8 is designed to read in three numbers that specify a range of temperatures, for all of which the luminous efficiency is to be computed and printed. The limits of the visible spectrum are also read in, so that these somewhat indefinite numbers can be varied if desired, and finally the number of intervals to be used in the integration is made part of the input.

begin real temp1, temp2, temp3, a, b, K, n, sum4, sum2, h, x, Percenteff;
Read (temp1, temp2, temp3, a, b, n);
h : = (b − a)/n;
for K : = temp1 **step** temp2 **until** temp3 **do**
    begin
    sum4 : = sum2 : = 0.0;
    for x : = a + h **step** 2 × h **until** b − 3 × h **do**
        begin
        sum4 : = sum4 + 1.0/(x ↑ 5 × (exp (1.432/(K × x)) − 1));
        sum2 : = sum2 + 1.0/((x + h) ↑ 5 × (exp (1.432/(K × (x + h))) − 1))
        end;
    Percenteff : = 64.77 × h/3 × (4 × sum4 + 2 × sum2 + 1.0/(a ↑ 5 × (exp (1.432/(K × a)) − 1))
        + 4.0/((b − h) ↑ 5 × (exp (1.432/(K × (b − h))) − 1))
        + 1.0/(b ↑ 5 × (exp (1.432/(K × b)) − 1)))/K ↑ 4;
    Print (K, Percenteff)
    end
end

Figure 4.8. Luminous efficiency program.

This program shows another example of a for-statement within a for-statement, with the two having entirely different purposes. The second for-statement carries out the summations of the integration; it is important here as always to be sure that the stopping value is precisely what is intended. We wish to compute $f(b − 3h)$ and $f(b − 2h)$ within the for-loop, leaving $f(b − h)$ and $f(b)$ to be computed afterward. Since the loop already contains an addition of h to the current value of the controlled variable, the proper stopping point is $b − 3h$, as shown.

It is a real annoyance to have to write out the formula of Planck's equation five times, as is done here. We shall see in Chapter 7 that there is an easy way out, whereby we write a *procedure body* in one place, then refer to it from as many different places in the program as necessary.

EXERCISES

1. Write statements or groups of statements to do the following. Complete program blocks are not required.

* a. Compute and print $y = x − \tan x$ for $x = 1.1$, 1.2, 1.3, $\cdots$, 1.9. Print both x and y for each value of x.

b. Compute and print for $x = 0.5, 0.7, 0.9, \cdots, 1.5$

$$y = x \tan \frac{x}{2} + 2 \ln \left| \cos \frac{x}{2} \right|$$

* c. Compute and print for $x = 0.1, 0.6, 0.7, 0.8, 0.9, 1.0$

$$y = \frac{1}{a\sqrt{a^2 + b^2}} \arctan \frac{a \tan x}{\sqrt{a^2 + b^2}}$$

d. Compute and print for $x = 1.0$, 1.05, 1.10, 1.15, 1.20, 1.25, 1.30, 1.45, 1.60

$$y = \frac{1}{4} \left(\frac{1}{a^4} − \frac{1}{x^4} \right) \arctan \frac{x}{a} − \frac{1}{12ax^3} + \frac{1}{4a^3 x}$$

* e. Given x, compute e^x from 20 terms of the infinite series

$$e^x = 1 + \frac{x}{1!} + \frac{x^2}{2!} + \frac{x^3}{3!} + \cdots$$

* f. Compute e^x from the infinite series, stopping after a term that is less than 10^{-6} times the sum so far.

g. Compute arctan x from the infinite series

$$\arctan x = x − \frac{x^3}{3} + \frac{x^5}{5} − \frac{x^7}{7} + − \cdots$$

stopping after a term that is less than 10^{-6} times the sum so far.

h. Compute π (to about four decimals) from

$$\frac{\pi}{4} = 1 − \tfrac{1}{3} + \tfrac{1}{5} − \tfrac{1}{7} + − \cdots$$

taking 500 terms. (Gregory's series.)

i. Compute π from

$$\frac{\pi}{4} = 4 \arctan \tfrac{1}{5} − \arctan \tfrac{1}{239}$$

In each arctangent stop after a term that is less than 10^{-7} times the sum so far.

* j. Compute π from the infinite product

$$\frac{\pi}{2} = \tfrac{2}{1} \cdot \tfrac{2}{3} \cdot \tfrac{4}{3} \cdot \tfrac{4}{5} \cdot \tfrac{6}{5} \cdot \tfrac{6}{7} \cdot \cdots$$

taking 150 factors. (Wallis' product.)

k. Compute and print $y = ae^{-bx}$ for $x = 0.1/b, 0.2/b, 0.3/b, \cdots, 3/b$. (You may use the exponential function.)

*l. Compute and print $y = ae^{-bx}$ for $x = 0.1$, 0.2, 0.3, $\cdots$, stopping when e^{-bx} is less than 0.001.

m. Compute $\sqrt[3]{A}$ by repeatedly applying the iteration formula

$$X_{i+1} = X_i + \frac{1}{3}\left(\frac{A}{X_i^2} - X_i\right)$$

stopping when two approximations are the same within 10^{-7} times the most recent.

*n. Compute and print

$$y = \sqrt{(\pi a)^2 + 1/b} + \frac{e^{-a/2}}{b + 6}$$

for all combinations of

$$a: 1.0(0.1)1.9$$
$$b: 1(1)20$$

where a: 1.0(0.1)1.9 means 1.0, 1.1, 1.2, $\cdots$, 1.9.

o. Compute and print

$$y = se^{-t^2 r^2} + t \ln \left| \cos \frac{\pi s}{t} \right|$$

for all combinations of

$$r: 0.01(0.005)0.5$$
$$s: 5(0.5)10$$
$$t: 1, 2, 3$$

2. Read values of α, t, and x from a card; then compute

$$\tau(x, t) = 50 - 4x - \frac{60}{\pi} \sum_{n=1}^{\infty} \frac{1}{n} e^{-4n^2\pi^2\alpha^2 t/100} \sin \frac{n\pi x}{5}$$

Stop computing terms of the infinite series as soon as the exponential factor becomes less than 10^{-5}. Compute all possible constant factors before going into the for-loop. Write as a complete block, with declarations.

*3. Write a program segment to print the value of N if N is a prime number and do nothing if N is not prime. N is odd.

A number is prime if it has no factors except 1 and itself. One way to determine whether N has any factors is to divide by the successive odd integers between 3 and $\sqrt{N}$, inclusive. If the remainder on division is ever zero, the number is not prime and we stop testing. If all remainders are nonzero, the number is prime.

A difficulty arises in that ALGOL does not provide the remainder on division.* With some extra effort, however, we can get it anyway, using the $\div$ operator. This operator, we recall, is defined only when both quantities are integers and produces a truncated integer quotient. Thus $23 \div 3 = 7$. Writing $Q = N \div D$, we can get the remainder from the formula

$$R = N - (N \div D) \times D.$$

---

*It is entirely feasible, however, to set up a special function to provide the remainder. It could be of the form mod (i, j), giving the remainder on dividing i by j. This useful function, or something equivalent, will probably be supplied in most processors.

For example, the remainder on division of 23 by 3 is
$$23 - (23 \div 3) \times 3 = 23 - 7 \times 3 = 2.$$
Similarly, the remainder on division of 36 by 3 is
$$36 - (36 \div 3) \times 3 = 36 - 12 \times 3 = 0.$$

We should give some thought to the method of stopping the loop that divides N by the successive odd integers between 3 and $\sqrt{N}$. It would be both awkward and unwise to make an actual test against $\sqrt{N}$ (which we would have to compute, of course). It would be unwise because the inherently approximate methods of a digital computer might not produce the exact square root of a perfect square. The "square root" of 25 could very well come out 4.9999999, which would lead to printing 25 as a prime. It would be awkward because there is a much simpler way: compare the square of the current divisor with N rather than the divisor itself with $\sqrt{N}$. This technique requires us to use a for-while construction in a rather simple program.

If you really want to compute primes, don't do it in ALGOL. The awkwardness in getting the remainders would be extremely costly in running time of the object program, among other problems. Such applications are probably best done in the language of the computer itself, that is, using machine-language coding.

4. Using the program segment of Exercise 3, write a complete program block to print all the primes from 5 to 5000. That is, use the earlier program to test 5, 7, 9, $\cdots$, 4999.

5. Write a complete program block to print a table of the natural logarithms of the numbers 2.00, 2.01, 2.02, $\cdots$, 5.00—without using the logarithm function.

There are many fairly simple series such as

$$\ln x = 2\left[\frac{x-1}{x+1} + \frac{(x-1)^3}{3(x+1)^3} + \frac{(x-1)^5}{5(x+1)^5} + \cdots\right]$$

to do this job. These converge slowly, however, and anyway there is a much better way. Use the series

$$\ln(x+a) = \ln x$$
$$+ 2\left[\frac{a}{2x+a} + \frac{a^3}{3(2x+a)^3} + \frac{a^5}{5(2x+a)^5} + \cdots\right]$$

where $x = 2.0$ initially and $a = 0.01$ ($\ln 2 = 0.69314718$). With these numbers the third term of the series is no greater than 10^{-13}, which would be completely lost when added to the first term, which is more like 10^{-3}. Therefore only two terms of the series need be taken and it is not even necessary to set up a loop to compute it.

6. A *truth table* of a Boolean expression lists the logical value of the function for all possible combinations of logical values of the variables appearing in the expression. For instance, the truth table of the expression $x = a \lor b$ is

a	b	x
False	False	False
False	True	True
True	False	True
True	True	True

If we let zero stand for False and 1 stand for True, this table can be presented a little more compactly as

a	b	x
0	0	0
0	1	1
1	0	1
1	1	1

Suppose we wanted to write a program to print a truth table. One way to do it (there are many others) would be to set up two nested for-statements to make the integers a and b both take on the values zero and one, then convert a and b to logical values, evaluate $x = a \lor b$, convert x back to an integer, and print. A program could be as shown in Figure 4.9.

Write a program to produce a truth table of the Boolean expression $y = a \land (b \lor \lnot c)$

7. Write a program to produce truth tables of the Boolean expressions

$$E1 = (\lnot A \land C \land \lnot E) \lor (\lnot A \land \lnot C \land D)$$

$$\lor (A \land C \land \lnot D \land \lnot E) \lor (\lnot A \land C \land D \land E)$$

$$E2 = (\lnot A \land D) \lor (C \land \lnot D \land \lnot E)$$

(The results of the executed programs should be the same.)

```
begin integer a, b, x; Boolean al, bl, xl;
for a : = 0, 1 do
for b : = 0, 1 do
      begin
      al : = if a = 1 then true else false;
      bl : = if b = 1 then true else false;
      xl : = al ∨ bl;
      x : = if xl then 1 else 0;
      Print (a, b, x)
      end
end
```

Figure 4.9. Program to compute a truth table.

5. SUBSCRIPTED VARIABLES

5.1 Introduction

Subscripted variables permit us to represent many quantities with one identifier. A particular one of the values is indicated by writing a subscript (or subscripts) in square brackets following the identifier. The complete set of quantities is called an *array*, and the individual quantities are called *elements* of the array. A subscripted variable may in principle have any number of subscripts. An array with one subscript is said to be one-dimensional, an array with two subscripts is said to be two-dimensional, etc. (When used in this connection, these terms refer to the number of *subscripts*, not to the number of *elements*: a one-dimensional array can have many elements, and a six-dimensional array could in principle have only one element—although there would be no point to such an array.) Any particular array has a fixed number of subscripts.

The first element of a one-dimensional array is frequently given the subscript 1, the second is number 2, etc., up to the number of elements in the array. In mathematical notation we might write x_1, x_2, x_3, $\cdots$, x_{19}, x_{20}; in ALGOL subscript notation we would write $x[1], x[2], x[3], \cdots, x[19], x[20]$.

Thus we see that the identifier x represents an entire array of elements; a particular element is specified by writing the identifier followed by brackets enclosing the number of a particular element. (We shall see that a subscript is not restricted to being a number but may in fact be any arithmetic expression.)

A two-dimensional array may be thought of as being composed of horizontal rows and vertical columns. The first of the two subscripts then refers to the *row number*, running (usually) from 1 up to the number of rows, and the second to the column number, running (usually) from 1 up to the number of columns. For instance, an array of two rows and three columns might be shown in mathematical notation as

$$A_{1,1} \quad A_{1,2} \quad A_{1,3}$$

$$A_{2,1} \quad A_{2,2} \quad A_{2,3}$$

In ALGOL subscript notation the elements could be written

$A[1, 1], A[1, 2], A[1, 3], A[2, 1], A[2, 2], A[2, 3]$

We note that the subscripts are separated by commas, as they are with three or more subscripts.

A three-dimensional array may be thought of, if one wishes, as being composed of planes, each plane containing rows and columns. The interpretation, however, depends somewhat on the purpose of the computation; other interpretations are possible.

As an example of the subscript notation, consider the problem of solving two simultaneous linear algebraic equations in two unknowns. To emphasize the similarity of subscripted variables with mathematical notation, we may write the system of equations completely in mathematical subscript form.

$$a_{1,1}x_1 + a_{1,2}x_2 = b_1$$

$$a_{2,1}x_1 + a_{2,2}x_2 = b_2$$

This problem can conveniently be set up with a one-dimensional array of two elements for the constant terms b_1 and b_2 and another for the unknowns x_1 and x_2 that we will compute. The coefficients (a's) will be the four elements of a two-dimensional array of two rows and two columns.

As with almost every problem, there are several ways to approach the solution of this system of equations. For our purposes here we may use Cramer's rule; a more widely applicable method is shown in Section 5.6. According to Cramer's rule, the solutions are

$$x_1 = \frac{b_1 \cdot a_{2,2} - b_2 \cdot a_{1,2}}{a_{1,1} \cdot a_{2,2} - a_{2,1} \cdot a_{1,2}}$$

$$x_2 = \frac{b_2 \cdot a_{1,1} - b_1 \cdot a_{2,1}}{a_{1,1} \cdot a_{2,2} - a_{2,1} \cdot a_{1,2}}$$

A program segment to evaluate these formulas is shown in Figure 5.1, in which we have done two things that should be explained. First, since the denominator of both expressions is the same, it is computed first and used in computing both x_1 and x_2. Second, there is a possibility that this denominator could be zero, indicating either no solution or an infinite number of solutions, depending on the constant terms. Either way, this formulation of the solution is not valid, since a division by zero would be required. (If division by zero is attempted in a computer, some sort of error indication is given, the nature of which depends on the machine and the particular version of ALGOL.) The program should test for this possibility.

Actually, we need to do a little more than just test the denominator for zero. Because of the rounding and truncation errors mentioned on page 17, the denominator could be very small—indicating trouble or at least inaccurate results—without actually being zero. We therefore test whether the absolute value of the denominator is less than some small number, taken arbitrarily to be 10^{-5} here. (In keeping with the discussion on page 39, it would in fact be much better to test for some sort of *relative* error.)

The preceding example showed only numerical subscripts. As we have noted, a subscript can be

denom := a [1, 1] × a [2, 2] − a [2, 1] × a [1, 2];
if abs (denom) $< _{10}-5$ **then** stop;
x [1] := (b [1] × a [2, 2] − b [2] × a [1, 2])/denom;
x [2] := (b [2] × a [1, 1] − b [1] × a [2, 1])/denom;

Figure 5.1. Program segment using subscripting to solve two simultaneous equations.

much more general: any arithmetic expression. The following illustration shows one use of arithmetic expressions in subscripts and another way that arrays can be viewed.

Suppose that at a certain point in a program the following computation is required:

$$y = \begin{cases} a + bx + cx^2 & \text{if } k = 1 \\ d + ex + fx^2 & \text{if } k = 2 \\ g + hx + ix^2 & \text{if } k = 3 \end{cases}$$

The values of x and k have already been established. We know how to write three assignment statements with different coefficients and then use if-statements to pick the appropriate statement, but the procedure is much simpler with subscripting.

Suppose we make the nine coefficients the elements of a one-dimensional array which we may call C and suppose we number the nine elements 3 to 11:

a	b	c	d	e	f	g	h	i
3	4	5	6	7	8	9	10	11

Now observe that if $k = 1$ the numbers of the desired elements are

$$3 = 3k$$

$$4 = 3k + 1$$

$$5 = 3k + 2$$

For $k = 2$, the numbers of the desired elements are

$$6 = 3k$$

$$7 = 3k + 1$$

$$8 = 3k + 2$$

For $k = 3$, the numbers are

$$9 = 3k$$

$$10 = 3k + 1$$

$$11 = 3k + 2$$

Thus, for any value of k, the proper coefficients will be used if we write

$$y := C[3 \times k] + C[3 \times k + 1] \times x$$
$$+ C[3 \times k + 2] \times x \uparrow 2$$

To illustrate once again that there is always another way to do anything, suppose the coefficients had been arranged thus:

$$\begin{array}{ccccccccc} a & d & g & b & e & h & c & f & i \\ 1 & 2 & 3 & 4 & 5 & 6 & 7 & 8 & 9 \end{array}$$

The assignment statement would then have been

$$y := C[k] + C[k+3] \times x + C[k+6] \times x \uparrow 2$$

Finally, the coefficients could be made the elements of a two-dimensional array, with rows and columns both being numbered from 1:

$$\begin{array}{ccc} a & b & c \\ d & e & f \\ g & h & i \end{array}$$

Now the assignment statement is

$$y := C[k, 1] + C[k, 2] \times x + C[k, 3] \times x \uparrow 2$$

This simple example shows in a variety of ways how subscripted variables facilitate the selection of one set of data from a larger set.

5.2   Array Declarations

When subscripted variables are used in a program, certain information must be supplied to the ALGOL processor:

1. Which variables are subscripted?
2. How many subscript positions are there for each subscripted variable, that is, what is the dimension of each?
3. How many elements are there in each array?
4. How are the elements numbered?

All of these questions are answered by an *array declaration* for each array. Every array, like every nonsubscripted variable, must be declared. This is done at the beginning of the block in which it is used, along with the type declarations and, as we shall see in later chapters, the switch and procedure declarations for the block.

Two definitions will simplify this discussion. A *bound pair* consists of two arithmetic expressions separated by a colon. A *bound pair list* consists of one or more bound pairs, separated by commas if there is more than one. Throughout this chapter, and in many practical applications, the bound pairs used in array declarations consist simply of two integers.

An array declaration for a single array consists of the word **array**, followed by the name of the array, followed by brackets enclosing as many bound pairs as there are subscript positions. Each bound pair specifies the range of values of the subscript in that position. For instance, a one-dimensional array named *coef* containing 15 elements numbered zero to 14 would be declared by

array coef [0:14];

The two-dimensional array used at the end of Section 5.1 would be declared by

array C [1:3, 1:3];

The lower bound (the first of a pair) must not be greater than the upper bound. Elements are always numbered consecutively in steps of 1 from the lower bound to the upper bound; that is, there is no provision for counting by twos or anything else but one. Subscripts may be negative.

The elements of a single array must all be of the same type, that is, real, integer, or Boolean. Real arrays may be declared by writing **array** or **real array**; integer arrays must be declared with **integer array**, and Boolean arrays with **Boolean array**. Notice that if the type of an array is not specifically identified, it is assumed to be real. (There is no such assumption for nonsubscripted variables.) When several arrays of the same type are to be declared, the words **array, real array, integer array,** or **Boolean array** need not be repeated. When several arrays of the same type and having the same bound pair list are to be declared, the bound pair list enclosed in brackets may be written only after the last group.

The following are acceptable array declarations.

array mu [1:100];
array kappa [−2:2];
array iota [−20:−10];
real array L [1:6, 0:24];
real array A [1:50], B [1:200], C [1:10, 1:10, 1:10];
array D, E, F, G [1:20, 1:20];
integer array data [−8:−3, −2:3, 29:57];
Boolean array Quine [1:30, 1:5];
Boolean array j, k, m [0:39], n [0:14], p, q [0:8];

Declarations for arrays of different types may be combined in any order; each declaration of a different type is considered to be a separate declaration and must therefore be set off by a semicolon. The following are acceptable declarations.

array X [1:10, 1:10], Y [0:49]; **integer array** I [−10:0];
Boolean array N [10:20]; **array** ABC [1:9, 0:10];
integer array ijk [0:5, 0:5, 0:5, 0:5, 1:10];
array BCD [1:2, 1:500];
array DEF [10:20]; **array** FEG [20:30]; **array** GHI [1:100];

We see from these examples, incidentally, that it is not *necessary* to take advantage of the various flexibilities in the manner of writing array declarations.

So much for the question of what information is conveyed by an array declaration and how it is written. What do we need to know about what the processor does with this information? The main point, for our purposes, is that an array declaration causes storage space to be reserved to hold the elements of the array. The processor must inspect the subscript bound pairs to determine how many dimensions there are and how many subscript positions there are in each dimension. On the basis of this information, enough storage locations can be set aside to hold the elements.

Thus we see that an array declaration causes the processor to take certain action in setting up the program, but it does not produce any action in the object program. This is true of all declarations.

One other processor action that results from an array declaration should be mentioned briefly. What is written in an array declaration has a significant influence on how the object program is set up to handle subscripted variables. A more precise statement of exactly what the processor does would require an extended discussion of processors for particular machines, which would be beyond the scope of this book. We may suggest, however, that the speed of the object program can in some cases depend rather strongly on such matters as whether arrays are numbered from one or from zero. In situations in which object program efficiency is important it would be well to obtain information on the characteristics of the source program with the most influence on object program efficiency. (This remark applies to other things than array declarations, but once again much depends on the particular computer and processor.)

5.3 Subscript Expressions

A subscript expression can be any arithmetic expression, including conditional expressions if desired. We saw examples of subscripts that were simple arithmetic expressions in Section 5.1.

Subscript expressions are most commonly written with integer quantities. If the value of a subscript expression is of type real, it is algebraically rounded to the nearest integer before being used as a subscript in picking out an element from the array. Thus A [2.4, 5.8, 6.5] leads to the same element as A [2, 6, 7] and B [1.89, −2.84, −7.5] leads to the same element as B [2, −3, −7].

In a great majority of practical applications all subscript expressions will be integers anyway, and the intricacies of the rounding of negative nonintegral expressions, etc., will never arise.

One of the common reasons for declaring a variable to be of type integer is that it will be used primarily in subscript expressions. This is done to improve the efficiency of object programs, since the conversion from the form in which real quantities are represented in most computers to the form in which integer quantities are represented takes a certain amount of time. Although it is frequently true that the results will be about the same, whether variables are real or integer, running time may be quite different.

Unless there is a specific reason to do otherwise, all variables and numbers appearing in subscript expressions should be of type integer, and quantities of types real and integer should not be mixed within one expression. These suggestions are for machine efficiency only, in most cases. On the other hand, any quantity that is not a whole number *must*, of course, be of type real.

5.4 Arrays and the for-Statement

The examples presented so far do not really indicate the power of subscript notation. There is nothing in the program for solving two simultaneous equations, for instance, that could not be done just as well by giving each variable a separate name. Why then are subscripted variables such an important feature of the ALGOL language?

The answer is that by using subscripts that are themselves variables we can set up a program in terms of a general element of one or more arrays, then perform the same computation on many elements by changing the value of the subscript. The modification of the variables in subscript expressions is most commonly done with for-statements; this use of the for-statement to manipulate elements of arrays is one of the most powerful aspects of ALGOL.

Suppose, for example, that we need to compute the sum of the squares of 20 numbers, x_1 to x_{20}, that have previously been stored in the computer. We could, of course, give them 20 different identifiers and write a long assignment statement to compute the sum of their squares, but this would be tedious, cumbersome, and inflexible. Instead, we set up the 20 numbers as the elements of a one-dimensional array which we may call x. Now, any of the 20 can be referenced by the subscripted identifier x [i], and we can arrange to let the subscript i run through all the values from 1 to 20.

The usual mathematical notation for this operation is

$$\text{sumsquares} = \sum_{i=1}^{20} x_i{}^2$$

The computation can be done with the program segment shown in Figure 5.2. We have included the array declaration here and have shown the program as a complete block to emphasize the necessity for a complete set of declarations in every program. After the declarations, the first step is to set *sumsquares* equal to zero so that we may use a single expression to compute each of the intermediate sums. Then we have a for-statement that causes i to take on the values 1 to 20 in succession, each time executing the one statement fol-

lowing the **do** of the **for.** Note that since there is only one controlled statement it does not have to be enclosed in statement parentheses. (See Figure 4.7, for instance, for a situation in which statement parentheses *are* required.)

A similar example is provided by the computation of the inner product of two vectors (one-dimensional arrays). Suppose the two arrays are named a and b and that each has ten elements numbered zero to nine. The mathematical definition of the problem is

$$\text{innerproduct} = \sum_{s=0}^{9} a_s b_s$$

A program segment to do this is shown in Figure 5.3. It presents no new concepts.

For a third example, consider the multiplication of a vector by a matrix. An $n \times n$ matrix consists of n^2 elements denoted by subscripts in precisely the same way as we have denoted the elements of a two-dimensional array. (The similarity is no accident, obviously: the ALGOL subscript notation was *designed* to be the same as matrix notation.) If we write the one-dimensional array (vector) by which the matrix is to be multiplied as a column vector, and the product also as a column vector, then the problem may be stated thus:

$$\begin{pmatrix} a_{11} & a_{12} & \cdots & a_{1n} \\ a_{21} & a_{22} & \cdots & a_{2n} \\ \cdots & \cdots & \cdots & \cdots \\ a_{n1} & a_{n2} & \cdots & a_{nn} \end{pmatrix} \begin{pmatrix} b_1 \\ b_2 \\ \cdot \\ \cdot \\ b_n \end{pmatrix} = \begin{pmatrix} c_1 \\ c_2 \\ \cdot \\ \cdot \\ c_n \end{pmatrix}$$

where

$$c_i = \sum_{j=1}^{n} a_{ij} b_j, \qquad i = 1, 2, \cdots, n$$

We see from this definition that the *first* element of the c-array is the sum of the products of the *first row* of the a-array and the elements of the b-array; the *second* element of c is the sum of the

---

```
begin real sumsquares; integer i; array x [1:20];
   sumsquares : = 0.0;
   for i : = 1 step 1 until 20 do sumsquares : = sumsquares + x [i] ↑ 2
   end
```

Figure 5.2. Program segment using subscripting and the for-statement to compute the sum of the squares of 20 numbers.

```
begin real innerproduct; array A, B [0:9]; integer s;
   innerproduct : = 0.0;
   for s : = 0 step 1 until 9 do innerproduct : = innerproduct + A [s] × B [s]
end
```

Figure 5.3. Program segment to compute the inner product of two vectors.

products of the *second* row of a and the elements of b; in general, the ith element of c is the sum of the products of the ith row of a and the elements of b.

An ALGOL program to produce the product array will evidently require two for-statements, one to form the sum of products and another to get each of the elements of the product array. The first for-statement will advance the i subscripts and the second the j subscripts. Saying it another way, during the execution of the second for-statement the subscript controlled by the first will be constant. The program is almost easier to write than to describe. In Figure 5.4 note that we have added one small refinement: the subscripts are all declared to range from 1 to 20 but the for-statements run until n. The idea here is that the arrays all have a maximum size but that there might be fewer than this maximum number of elements in them. For instance, if the a-array contains only 100 elements in a 10 by 10 segment of its 400 storage positions and the b-array has only ten elements, we can set $n = 10$ and carry out the computation correctly for that case. It is assumed here that the value of n is established by a statement not shown. This kind of flexibility will be elaborated in Chapter 6.

Also note in Figure 5.4 that the assignment statement to set each element of c equal to zero is included in the range of the first for-statement. This clearing to zero will thus be carried out once for each time through the for-loop that controls the i subscript.

5.5 Case Study 5: Determining a Median

We are given a frequency distribution of the weekly earnings of the employees of a factory in a form like that shown in Table 5.1.

The *median* of such a distribution is defined as the salary that divides the employees into two equal groups, half earning less and half earning more. For the data shown the median is $57.69, computed by the following method (which is itself an algorithm of sorts).

1. Divide N, the total number of employees, by 2, which gives the number that must lie on each side of the median to be found.

TABLE 5.1

Weekly Earnings		Number
0–$	20.00	17
$ 20.00–	29.99	48
30.00–	39.99	70
40.00–	44.99	53
45.00–	49.99	67
50.00–	54.99	94
55.00–	59.99	129
60.00–	69.99	142
70.00–	79.99	92
80.00–	89.99	55
90.00–	99.99	36
100.00–	200.00	34

```
begin integer i, j, n; array a [1:20, 1:20], b, c [1:20];
for i : = 1 step 1 until n do
      begin
      c [i] : = 0.0;
      for j : = 1 step 1 until n do c [i] : = c [i] + a [i, j] × b [j]
      end
end
```

Figure 5.4. Program segment to form the product of a matrix and a vector.

2. Begin at the lower end of the distribution and add together the number of employees in the successive classes until reaching the class containing the median.

3. Determine the number of employees from this class that must be added to the total of all the preceding classes to give $N/2$.

4. Divide the additional number thus required by the number of employees in the class containing the median. This indicates the fractional part of the class-interval within which the required cases lie.

5. Multiply the class-interval by this fraction.

6. Add the result of this multiplication to the lower limit of the interval containing the median, giving the median.

The last four steps amount to a simple interpolation.

We may generalize the problem statement somewhat in order to make it apply to a wider class of data and to make it more suitable for computer solution. Suppose we limit the number of class-intervals to 100. We can then set up two one-dimensional arrays to hold the definitions of the intervals and the number in each interval. It might seem that each interval would require two numbers to define it, but we can get by with one if an additional assumption is justified: there are no gaps between intervals. This allows us to store only the upper limit of each interval, since the lower limit of the next interval must always be one cent more. (Storing only the lower limit would also be possible, of course.)

Let us call the array containing the upper limits of the intervals *class* and the array containing the number in each class *freq*, for frequency. It is essential that the data be placed in these arrays in corresponding positions so that the first element of *class* will correspond to the first element of *freq*,

etc. It is also essential that the data be arranged in ascending sequence, as in the example.

We shall assume that a value has been given to a variable named *number;* this specifies how many intervals (and corresponding frequencies) there actually are. It will, in general, be less than the maximum of 100. Thus our program will be able to handle any data as long as there are no more than 100 classes; this kind of generality is typical of computer programs.

We may now begin to investigate what is involved in writing an ALGOL program to follow the six-step procedure outlined above. The first thing will be to find the total of the frequencies in the *freq* array. This is easily done with a simple for-loop. After dividing this total by 2, we begin looking for the interval in which the median must lie. This may conveniently be done with another summing loop, this time based on the for-while construction. The Boolean expression will be written to stop the loop as soon as adding the frequency for one more class interval would take us past the halfway point of the total. Once we get out of this loop we can subtract the total of the preceding classes from the halfway point, divide the difference by the number in the next class, multiply by the class-interval of that class, and add the lower limit of that class—giving the median.

A program to do all this is shown in Figure 5.5, in which there are only two features that should require elaboration. As always in a for-loop that is terminated by exhaustion of the for-list, the value of the controlled variable will be undefined upon exit. Yet the value of the subscript upon termination is needed to determine which class contains the median. The solution is to set another variable, named j, equal to the controlled variable each time the compound statement following the **do** is executed.

The second point requiring careful attention is

```
begin integer i, j, number; real sum, midpoint, median; array class, freq [1:100];
    sum : = 0.0;
    for i : = 1 step 1 until number do sum : = sum + freq [i];
    midpoint : = sum/2.0;
    sum : = 0.0;
    for i : = 0, i + 1 while sum + freq [i] < midpoint do
        begin sum : = sum + freq [i]; j : = i end;
    median : = (midpoint − sum)/freq [j + 1] × (class [j + 1] − class [j]) + class [j] + 0.01
end
```

Figure 5.5. Program to compute a median.

the precise value of the variable j after exiting from the loop: does it specify the class containing the median or the one before it? A good practice at this point is to work with a small example. Suppose there were only three elements in each array, with sample data as follows:

Class	Frequency
0.00–19.99	2
20.00–29.99	12
30.00–39.99	6

For this sample, the second for-loop would terminate with $j = 1$, the number of the class *before* the one containing the median, since adding the frequency for the next interval would take us past the midpoint. In terms of j, the number in the *next* class—the one containing the midpoint—is freq $[j + 1]$. The class interval of the next class—20.00 to 29.99 in the sample—is given by class $[j + 1]$ − class $[j]$. (Remember that we stored the *upper* limit of each class.) The lower limit of the next class is given by class $[j] + 0.01$.

With the necessary logic worked out, the program in Figure 5.5 is not difficult. The logic is not exactly obvious, however, and the reader is urged to satisfy himself that the program actually does compute a median. Try out the program on a small set of sample data by working through on paper just what the program would do at each point. (This is an excellent idea in checking any program.)

It will be noted that there are no input or output operations here. These have been omitted simply because we are concentrating on other things.*

5.6 Case Study 6: Simultaneous Linear Algebraic Equations

A program is to be set up to solve a system of simultaneous linear algebraic equations. The pro-

---

* But we cannot this time fall back on the phrase "values are assumed to have been assigned by previous sections of the program, and later sections will use the results." We shall see in Chapter 6, in discussing block structure, that all the variables declared in a block are *local* to that block and thereby become inaccessible in any higher level block. To make a usable program of this example, it would be necessary either to include the input and output operations in *this* block or to declare the input and output variables in a *higher level* block.

gram should be able to solve a system of any number of equations, up to some maximum imposed by the amount of storage available in the computer. We shall arbitrarily take 50 equations as the maximum number that the program will be able to handle.

Among the many methods for solving such a system, we choose the Seidel iteration method, which applies if the coefficients of the unknowns meet the following restriction: the main diagonal coefficient in each row must *dominate* the other coefficients in the row, which is true if

$$|A_{ii}| > \sum_{i \neq j} |A_{ij}|, \qquad i = 1, 2, \cdots, n$$
$$n = \text{number of equations}$$

(Less stringent conditions are actually sufficient, but a discussion of them is beyond the scope of this book.)

The Seidel iteration method will find the solution (if there is one, of course) to any system meeting this restriction, but it will be particularly advantageous if either or both of the following additional conditions are satisfied:

1. An approximate solution is known in advance.
2. Most of the coefficients are zero. (If the array has special characteristics, such as all zeros above the main diagonal, much better methods are available.)

The essence of the Seidel iteration method is to make a guess at the values of the unknowns and then to improve the approximation repeatedly. With the restriction stated above, the successive approximations will converge to the true values of the unknowns, no matter what initial guess is taken. We may illustrate the process with a system of three equations:

$$a_{11}x_1 + a_{12}x_2 + a_{13}x_3 = b_1$$
$$a_{21}x_1 + a_{22}x_2 + a_{23}x_3 = b_2$$
$$a_{31}x_1 + a_{32}x_2 + a_{33}x_3 = b_3$$

If there is any information available about the expected values of the unknowns, then such values should be used. The closer the initial guesses to the final values, the fewer the number of iterations that will be required. Lacking such information, we may use any values, typically zero for each variable.

We begin by computing a new value of x_1 from

the first equation. With a prime to denote a new value of an unknown, we may write

$$x_1' = (b_1 - a_{12}x_2 - a_{13}x_3)/a_{11}$$

Using this new value of x_1 and the old value of x_3, we compute a new value for x_2 from equation 2:

$$x_2 = (b_2 - a_{21}x_1' - a_{23}x_3)/a_{22}$$

Using the new values of x_1 and x_2, we compute a new value of x_3 from equation 3:

$$x_3 = (b_3 - a_{31}x_1' - a_{32}x_2')/a_{33}$$

This gives us a new approximation to the values of the unknowns, which constitutes one iteration. As many iterations are taken as are required to obtain two successive approximations to the unknowns that are "sufficiently close" to each other. Various definitions of closeness are used; here, on each iteration we will form the sum of the absolute values of the difference between each new value of the unknowns and the previous value of the unknowns. The measure of the difference between two sets of unknowns, which is called the *norm*, is thus given by

$$\text{Norm} = \sum_{i=1}^{n} |x_i - x_i'|$$

What this means in programming terms is that before storing the new value of each unknown we must form the absolute value of the difference between it and the previous value of that unknown and add to the norm. At the end of each iteration we will determine whether the norm is less than a test constant that has been read in as input to the program. If it is, then the unknowns have been computed to sufficient accuracy; if not, we must make another iteration.

One of the most challenging aspects of a program like this is the question of getting the data into the computer. With the assumption of a maximum of 50 equations, there could be as many as 2600 numbers to enter: $50 \cdot 50 = 2500$ coefficients, 50 constant terms, and 50 guesses to the unknowns. If it should happen, as is not unlikely, that many of the coefficients are zero, the program should be able to accept only nonzero quantities. We must bypass this interesting question, however, since we have not yet considered the details of input and output. The interested reader is invited to preview Chapter 8 or to consult the manual on his version of ALGOL.

The program of Figure 5.6 is an extension of the short example above to the general case of n equations. The major for-loop computes a new value of one unknown each time it is executed. Its controlled variable, i, picks out one equation, which is the same for all executions of the inner for-loop. This for-loop is the first realistic example of a for-statement with more than one for-list. The first for-list gets the products to the left of the main diagonal term, and the second gets all products to its right. It is always a good idea to check carefully whether a statement of this sort operates correctly on the first and last equations: in the first there is no term to the left of the diagonal, and in the last there is none to the right. The way the execution of the for-statement is defined, however, we encounter no difficulty. Since the test for computation is made before executing the con-

```
        begin real sum, norm, tempx, test; integer i, j, n; array b, x [1:50], a [1:50, 1:50];
again:  norm := 0.0;
        for i := 1 step 1 until n do
            begin
            sum := 0.0;
            for j := 1 step 1 until i − 1, i + 1 step 1 until n do
                sum := sum + a [i, j] × x [j];
            tempx := (b [i] − sum)/a [i, i];
            norm := norm + abs (tempx − x [i]);
            x [i] := tempx
            end;
        if norm < test then stop else go to again
        end
```

Figure 5.6. Program for solution of a system of simultaneous equations by the Seidel iteration method. (Input and output operations not shown.)

trolled statement, the first for-list will have no effect when $i = 1$ and the last will have no effect when $i = n$.

This brings up a worthwhile digression. If it were not for the fact that the ALGOL for-statement is as flexible as it is, we might have been tempted to form the sum of the products for the entire row, including the main diagonal term, and then subtract off the diagonal term after getting out of the for-loop. It would seem that this would be no more than an application of the obvious equation $a + b - b = a$. This unfortunately is not always true in a computer. Consider the following example:

$$0.00005782$$

$$+974286.35$$

$$-974286.35$$

Consider now what happens when the addition is performed. In any computer we can maintain only a finite number of places, typically eight in an ALGOL real quantity. With the data shown, the addition creates a sum having 14 significant digits; if the computer can hold only eight, the sum must be rounded, giving 974286.35 as the sum. The smaller number has been lost entirely. When the larger number is subtracted from this "sum," the result is zero!

This is an extreme example, of course, but even when the difference in size is not so great there can still be partial loss of significance. Consideration of this problem must be a major concern in programming any application in which it could arise. It is not at all difficult to "solve" a large system of equations and arrive at a set of values for the unknowns having *no significant places whatsoever*. And it is easy to overlook this consideration, since the answers may be printed with eight or ten digits and still mean next to nothing. To see how this can happen, consider the expression

$$(1.2345678 - 2.3345678) \times 8.7654321$$

The result might be printed as 9.6419753, yet it has exactly *two* significant digits.

The situation is usually not quite so dire as this, but the reader will still do well to exercise caution in accepting a computer result as being accurate to the number of places printed. (Analysis of errors of this and other kinds is one of the most important and most interesting aspects of numerical analysis.)

Turning again to the program, we may note a few more instructive features. The assignment statement for *tempx* contains a subscripted variable in which both subscripts are the same. This is perfectly legitimate; what we want here is to obtain the diagonal element from whatever equation we are in, and the subscripting shown does just that. The following statement adds to the error sum the difference between the new value of the unknown just computed and the old value of that unknown. The absolute value function is used to discard the sign of the difference. After the difference has been added to the norm, we store the new value in the location for the unknown. After getting out of the outer for-loop, which completes one iteration, we have an if-statement to determine whether the process has converged within the limit set by the value of the variable *test*. If we have finished, we would normally go on to print the values of the unknowns; the output statements are not shown here.

This program, with input and output statements added, was run on a computer using the system of five equations shown in Figure 5.7. Zeros were used for the initial guesses. The exact answers are 1, -2, 3, -4, and 5. The machine output is shown in Figure 5.8, where the approximations to the five unknowns are listed across the page, followed by the norm. The test for convergence was 0.1.

EXERCISES

1. Write program segments to do the following. Make each program a block, including array declarations. All

$$12.418x_1 - 1.061x_2 + 2.669x_3 + 4.361x_4 - 0.119x_5 = 4.508$$
$$-1.501x_1 + 19.832x_2 + 0.694x_3 - 4.816x_4 + 2.274x_5 = -8.449$$
$$2.308x_1 + 1.728x_2 - 15.165x_3 - 2.023x_4 + 1.104x_5 = -33.031$$
$$3.359x_1 - 0.913x_2 - 6.441x_3 + 27.864x_4 + 3.737x_5 = -106.909$$
$$-1.562x_1 + 1.168x_2 - 2.004x_3 + 1.818x_4 + 9.490x_5 = 30.268$$

Figure 5.7. The system of equations used to test the program of Figure 5.6 and which produced the output of Figure 5.8.

subscripts should be numbered from 1, unless there is a definite advantage to you in doing otherwise.

*a. The coordinates of a point in space are given by the three elements of a one-dimensional array named x. (Note the different usages of the word dimension: the elements of a one-dimensional array are the coordinates of a point in three-dimensional space!) Compute the distance from the origin to the point.

b. Given a two-dimensional array named R, the elements of which are to be viewed as the elements of a 3 x 3 determinant, compute the value of the determinant, which should be named det. (Use any method you know, without trying to develop a general method for finding the value of an n x n determinant.)

*c. Two one-dimensional arrays named a and b each contain 30 elements. Compute

$$D = \sum_{i=1}^{30} (a_i - b_i)^2$$

d. Two one-dimensional arrays named x and y each contain 45 elements. Compute

$$N = \left(\sum_{i=1}^{45} x_i y_i \right)^{1/2}$$

*e. A one-dimensional array named $data$ contains 78 elements. Compute the sum of every third element, beginning with the second.

f. A one-dimensional array named G contains 64 elements. Form the sum of the first, fourth, ninth, sixteenth, twenty-fifth, thirty-sixth, forty-ninth, and sixty-fourth elements.

g. A one-dimensional array named x contains 50 elements. Compute the 49 elements of another array named $firstdiffx$, according to

firstdiffx [i] = x [i + 1] − x [i], i = 1, 2, 3, ···, 49

*h. A one-dimensional array named Y contains 32 elements. Compute

trapezoidal $= Y_1 + 2Y_2 + 2Y_3$

$$+ \cdots + 2Y_{30} + 2Y_{31} + Y_{32}$$

i. A two-dimensional array named $amatrix$ contains ten rows and ten columns. A one-dimensional array named $adiagonal$ contains ten elements. Compute the elements of $adiagonal$ from

adiagonal [i] = amatrix [i,i]

*j. Given two one-dimensional arrays named a and b, each containing 23 elements. If every $a_i > b_i$, for $i = 1, 2, 3, \cdots, 23$, assign the logical value **true** to a Boolean variable named $greater$; otherwise, assign it the logical value **false.**

*k. A one-dimensional array named $vector$ contains 20 elements, numbered from 1. Place the element that is algebraically largest in Big and its element number in Nbig. *Hint.* Place the first element in Big and place a 1 in Nbig, then compare Big with the other 19 elements in succession. Each time an element is found that is larger than Big, place *it* in big and its element number in Nbig.

l. Using the scheme of the previous exercise, exchange the first and the largest element of the array named $vector$.

*m. The two previous exercises form the basis of a scheme to *sort* the elements of the array named vector into descending sequence. After exchanging the *first* and the largest, go on to exchange the *second* and the largest of those remaining, then the *third* and the largest of the remaining, etc. (Naturally, if the element in any position is already the largest of those remaining, the exchange is not performed.)

n. Sort the 37 elements of a one-dimensional array named $list$ into ascending (note change) sequence of absolute values.

*o. An array named $influence$ has seven rows and 17 columns. Place the algebraically largest element of $influence$ in $heavy$, the row number of $heavy$ in row, and the column number of $heavy$ in $column$.

p. A one-dimensional integer array named M contains 20 elements numbered from 1. Replace each element of M by itself, multiplied by its element number. In other words, replace m_i by $i \cdot m_i$.

*q. Two one-dimensional arrays named R and S have a *maximum* of 40 elements each. The *actual* number of elements in each is given by the value of a previously computed integer M. Compute the first M elements of an array named T, which also has a maximum of 40 elements, according to

T [i] = R [i] + S [i]   i = 1, 2, 3, ···, M

*r. A one-dimensional array named F contains at most 50 elements to be *smoothed*, as follows. Each of the first M elements, except the first and Mth, is to be replaced by

$$F_i = \frac{F_{i-1} + F_i + F_{i+1}}{3}$$

.363	−.398	2.187	−3.387	4.409	10.746
1.090	−1.748	2.917	−3.942	4.955	3.908
1.018	−1.976	2.994	−3.996	4.998	.474
1.002	−1.998	2.999	−4.000	5.000	.048

Figure 5.8. Output of the program of Figure 5.6, using the system of equations in Figure 5.7 as input.

As soon as a new value of an element has been computed, that new value is to be used in the computation of the new value of the next element.

s. The same as the previous exercise, except use only *old* values of all elements.

*t. Two one-dimensional arrays named X and Y contain 50 elements each. A variable named xs is known to be equal to one of the elements of X. If $xs = X_i$, place Y_i in ys.

u. In a certain problem Y is given as an empirical step function of X, according to a set of formulas:

if

$$x < a_1, \quad y = y_1$$
$$a_1 < x \leqq a_2, \quad y = y_2$$
$$a_2 < x \leqq a_3, \quad y = y_3$$
$$\cdots \cdots \cdots \cdots$$
$$a_{20} < x \quad , \quad y = y_{21}$$

Set up appropriate arrays and a program to find y when x is given.

v. Two one-dimensional arrays named x and y contain 50 elements each. The elements in x form a monotonic ascending sequence, that is, $x_{i+1} > x_i$, $i = 1, 2, 3, \cdots, 49$. If $xt < x_1$ or $xt > x_{50}$, transfer to statement 4190. If $xt = x_i$ for any i, place y_i in yt. Otherwise, find two elements of the x array such that $x_{i-1} < xt < x_i$ and compute yt from

$$yt = y_{i-1} + \frac{y_i - y_{i-1}}{x_i - x_{i-1}} (xt - x_{i-1})$$

(Linear interpolation.)

w. Two one-dimensional arrays named x and y contain 60 elements each. The y array is expected to have exactly one *local maximum*, that is, three elements such that

$$y_{i-1} < y_i > y_{i+1}$$

If there is no local maximum, place a zero in *number;* if there is more than one, place a 2 in *number;* if there is exactly 1, place a 1 in *number*, place x_i in xloc, and place i in *where*.

*x. Three two-dimensional arrays, a, b, and c, have 15 rows and 15 columns each. Compute the elements of c according to

$$c_{ij} = \sum_{k=1}^{15} a_{ik}b_{kj} \qquad i, j = \quad 1, 2, \cdots, 15$$

y. A two-dimensional array, *rst*, has 25 rows and 25 columns. Compute the product of the main diagonal elements of *rst* and place it in *diagprod*. A main diagonal element is one that has the same row and column number.

2. Given a 30 x 30 array named *coef* and two one-dimensional arrays named b and x, together with an integer variable named n. *Coef* and b are to be regarded as the coefficients and the constant terms of the specialized system of simultaneous equation:

$$a_{11}x_1 \qquad\qquad\qquad = b_1$$
$$a_{21}x_1 + a_{22}x_2 \qquad\qquad = b_2$$
$$a_{31}x_1 + a_{32}x_i + a_{33}x_3 \qquad = b_3$$
$$\cdots \cdots \cdots \cdots \cdots \cdots \cdots$$
$$a_{n1}x_1 + a_{n2}x_2 + a_{n3}x_3 + \cdots + a_{nn}x_n = b_n$$

Compute the values of the n unknowns.

3. The elements of a two-dimensional array named u are to be regarded as the values of a function at the mesh-points of a rectangular grid. The array has a maximum of 40 rows and 40 columns, with the actual number for a particular solution being given by the values of the integer variables m and n, respectively. Each of the *interior* points of the arrays is to be replaced by

$$u_{ij} = \frac{u_{i-1,j} + u_{i+1,j} + u_{i,j-1} + u_{i,j+1}}{4}$$

As each new interior point is computed, form the absolute value of the difference between the new and old values of u_{ij}; form the sum of all of these *residues*. The computation of a new value of u_{ij} at all interior points and the computation of the sum of all residues is called a *sweep* of the grid. Sweep the grid as many times as necessary to produce a sum of residues on one sweep that is less than 0.01. (One method of iterative solution of Laplace's equation.)

4. Given two one-dimensional arrays named *length* and *angle*, each containing a maximum of 15 elements. The elements are to be regarded as the lengths and angles of a supposedly closed polygon, as shown in Figure 5.9. You do not know how many sides the polygon has; this will be signaled by the first "length" of zero as the *length* array is scanned. Compute *closureerror*, the amount by which the polygon fails to close.

5. Refer to Exercise 16 of Chapter 1. Suppose that the letters of the two words are represented by the elements of two one-dimensional arrays, in which the letters have been coded in some numerical form. Place in *common* the number of letters common to both words.

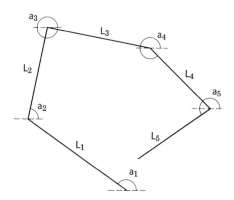

Figure 5.9. Polygon having, in general, n sides, for Exercise 4. All angles are measured from the horizontal and are in degrees.

6. Boolean variables and Boolean equations are heavily used in designing logic circuits for computers. In such work it is frequently necessary to find the simplest Boolean expression that is equivalent to a given expression. This exercise explores part of one method for doing so.

Two Boolean arrays named Quine1 and Quine2 each contain ten rows and five columns. First compare row 1 and row 2 of Quine1, examining each pair of elements for *equivalence*. (Two Boolean variables are equivalent if they are both true or both false. See page 29.) If exactly one pair of the Boolean variables in the two rows is *not* equivalent, we shall say that the two rows *combine*. For instance, writing *T* for true and *F* for false, these two rows combine:

$$T \quad T \quad F \quad T \quad F$$
$$T \quad F \quad F \quad T \quad F$$

So do these:

$$T \quad F \quad T \quad F \quad T$$
$$T \quad F \quad T \quad F \quad F$$

These two do not combine:

$$T \quad F \quad T \quad T \quad T$$
$$F \quad T \quad T \quad T \quad T$$

Neither do these:

$$T \quad T \quad F \quad F \quad T$$
$$T \quad T \quad F \quad F \quad T$$

(You may assume that this last will never happen, if it matters to your method of solution, because of the way Quine1 would have been generated.)

Compare the first row with all the other rows in this manner. If the first row does not combine with any other row, move the first row of Quine1 to the first row of Quine2. Similarly, compare the second row of Quine1 with the third and all following rows of Quine1 and move it to Quine2 if it combines with none of them, finally comparing the ninth row with the tenth row.

You will move from one to nine rows of Quine1 to Quine2, depending on how the comparisons turn out. The rows of Quine2 should be filled *in order*; that is, if the first row of Quine1 combines but the second does not, then the second row of Quine1 should be moved to the *first* row of Quine2, etc.

You will find it advantageous to employ four variable subscripts: one for the row number of Quine1 being compared with all following, another for the row number following, one for the column number of either array, and one for the row number of Quine2.

Place in *count* the number of rows moved to Quine2.

7. The program in Figure 5.5 will not work if the median lies in the first class interval. Why not? Does the same problem arise if the median lies in the last class interval? Rewrite the program to avoid this problem.

6. SWITCHES AND BLOCKS

6.1 Switches

An ALGOL *switch* is an extension of the idea of a conditional transfer of control; it allows us to transfer to any one of a number of statements, depending on the value of an arithmetic expression.

Suppose, for example, that it is necessary to transfer to one of the statements labeled L1, S, 67, 43, and L3, depending on whether the value of the integer i is 1, 2, 3, 4, or 5, respectively. We already know how to do this with a long if-statement:

if $i = 1$ **then go to** L1 **else if** $i = 2$ **then**
go to S **else if** $i = 3$ **then go to** 67
else if $i = 4$ **then go to** 43
else if $i = 5$ **then go to** L3;

This could also be done with a go to statement having a long if-clause:

go to if $i = 1$ **then** L1 **else if** $i = 2$ **then** S
else **if** $i = 3$ **then** 67 **else if** $i = 4$
then 43 **else** L3;

Either way is cumbersome; it is much better to set up a switch to do the same thing much more compactly and efficiently. The switch is *established* by declaring it:

switch S : = L1, S4, 67, 43, L3

It can then be *used* to do what the long conditional statement does, simply by writing

go to S[i]

A switch may be thought of as analogous to a one-dimensional array, in which the "elements" are not values but labels. Writing the name of the switch followed by brackets enclosing an arithmetic expression designates the kth label of the switch, where k is the integer nearest the value of the expression. (In most cases the arithmetic expression will, in fact, be a single integer variable.) The labels in a switch declaration are taken to be numbered from 1 upward; in contrast to arrays, there is no way to specify that the numbering start with anything but 1. This is occasionally a bit awkward but rather easily compensated for, as we shall see.

Switch declarations must appear in the heading of a block, along with the type declarations (real, integer, or Boolean), the array declarations, and one or two other kinds of declarations. The switch may then be used anywhere in the program.*

For an example of one way in which a switch may be utilized, consider the following problem. We are required to compute one of the first five Legendre polynomials, given values of *legno* and x:

If *legno* = 0, $P_0(x) = 1$

$= 1, P_1(x) = x$

$= 2, P_2(x) = \frac{3}{2}x^2 - \frac{1}{2}$

$= 3, P_3(x) = \frac{5}{2}x^3 - \frac{3}{2}x$

$= 4, P_4(x) = \frac{35}{8}x^4 - \frac{15}{4}x^2 + \frac{3}{8}$

---

* More precisely, anywhere that the declaration is valid and defined, in the case of more complex block structures. See Section 6.2.

go to poly [legno + 1];
P0: legendre : = 1.0; **go to** next;
P1: legendre : = x; **go to** next;
P2: legendre : = 1.5 × x ↑ 2 − 0.5; **go to** next;
P3: legendre : = 2.5 × x ↑ 3 − 1.5 × x; **go to** next;
P4: legendre : = 4.375 × x ↑ 4 − 3.75 × x ↑ 2 + 0.375; **go to** next;
next

Figure 6.1. Program using a switch to compute a Legendre polynomial.

Let *Legendre* be the name of the polynomial to be calculated. The job is done fairly readily with a switch. In the head of the appropriate block we place the switch declaration

switch poly : = P0, P1, P2, P3, P4;

The name *poly* has been made up for the switch, together with the labels shown for the five statements that will compute the appropriate polynomial. Figure 6.1 shows an ALGOL program segment to find the desired result. The first statement causes a transfer to one of the following five. With *poly* having been declared a switch, the statement

go to poly [legno + 1]

will transfer to the statement with the *k*th label in the declaration, where *k* is the integer nearest *legno* + 1. Since *legno* runs from zero to four (not one to five), this arrangement does precisely what we want.

Another example of switch usage appears in Section 6.6.

6.2 Block Structure

We have noted earlier that an ALGOL program is always a *block*, a block being one or more statements enclosed between the statement parentheses **begin** and **end** and containing declarations immediately following the **begin**. We shall now explore a more complex (and more typical) program organization in which the over-all program block contains other blocks.

The fundamental concept is that of *local* and *global* identifiers. Consider the schematic diagram of a program shown in Figure 6.2. The variables *a*, *b*, and *c* are *local* to block B1, which contains blocks B2 and B3 as *sub-blocks*. The variables

d and *e* are local to B2, and the variables *f* and *g* are local to B3. The variables *a*, *b*, and *c* are *global* to blocks B2 and B3. Variables *d* and *e* are neither local nor global to block B3, and *f* and *g* are neither local nor global to B2. Blocks B2 and B3 are said to be independent.

Let us generalize these examples. Suppose first that a block B2 is a sub-block of B1.

1. Any variable that is declared in B1 and not in B2 is local to B1 and global to B2.

2. Any variable that is declared in B2 is local to B2 and *undefined* in B1. This means that a statement in B1 cannot refer to any identifier declared in B2 because such an identifier is unknown outside of B2.

Suppose next that blocks B2 and B3 are independent of each other, that is, neither is a sub-block of the other.

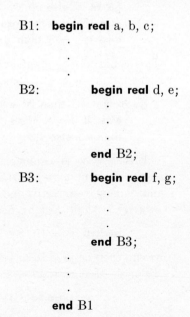

B1:   **begin real** a, b, c;
          .
          .
          .
B2:   **begin real** d, e;
                .
                .
                .
          end B2;
B3:   **begin real** f, g;
                .
                .
                .
          end B3;
          .
          .
          .
       end B1

Figure 6.2. Schematic representation of a block structure.

TABLE 6.1

Vari-able	Block						
	C1	C2	C3	C4	C5	C6	C7
r	Local	Global	Global	Global	Global	Global	Global
s	Undefined	Local	Global	Global	Undefined	Undefined	Undefined
t	Undefined	Undefined	Local	Undefined	Undefined	Undefined	Undefined
w	Undefined	Undefined	Undefined	Local	Undefined	Undefined	Undefined
x	Undefined	Undefined	Undefined	Undefined	Local	Undefined	Undefined
y	Undefined	Undefined	Undefined	Undefined	Undefined	Local	Global
z	Undefined	Undefined	Undefined	Undefined	Undefined	Undefined	Local

3. Any identifier declared in one block is undefined in any block that is independent of it.

From a practical programming standpoint, the important question is where is an identifier defined; that is, when is it possible to use an identifier in a statement? We may attempt a generalization as follows:

An identifier is defined in any block in which it is local or global, and not otherwise.

We may illustrate these ideas with a more comprehensive example, shown in Figure 6.3. Table 6.1 summarizes the ways in which statements in one block may refer to identifiers declared in other blocks. A note of caution: when we say "a statement *in* block C1," for instance, we mean *in* block C1 but *not* in any of its sub-blocks.

One important concept of block structure is that of where an identifier is defined; a second is the matter of retention of values of variables declared in a block:

After leaving a block, the values of all variables declared in that block are lost; upon re-entry into the block, their values are undefined.*

This may appear at first glance to be a pointless restriction; actually, it is the major reason for bothering with the complications of block structure at all because it permits more than one variable to be allocated to the same computer storage location. This can be crucial in doing a job requiring a great deal of storage.

Consider the structure shown in Figure 6.3 again. Since values are not preserved on leaving a block,

*This rule can be bypassed with the *own* declaration. See Section 6.4.

the variables t, w, and z can all be stored in the same location; the three are never defined at the same time. Similarly, s, x, and y are never defined at the same time and can be stored in the same place. The variables s and t cannot be assigned to the same location, on the other hand, because there is a time when both are defined, namely during the execution of block C3. ALGOL processors are designed to recognize these possibilities and assign storage accordingly.

The computers used with ALGOL typically have storage for many thousands of numbers, so that this consideration is not of great importance for single variables. With arrays, it can be decisive.

We may conclude this part of the discussion of blocks by noting that statement labels are always local to the block in which they appear. In other

```
C1:   begin real r;
C2:       begin real s;
C3:           begin real t;
              end C3;
C4:           begin real w;
              end C4;
          end C2;

C5:       begin real x;
          end C5;
C6:       begin real y;
C7:           begin real z;
              end C7;
          end C6;
      end C1
```

Figure 6.3. Schematic representation of a more complex block structure.

words, a label is considered to have been "declared" in the block in which it is written. There are two important consequences of this fact. First, there is no problem of duplication of labels in different blocks; this is perfectly acceptable and will cause no problems to the processor. Second, it is impossible to transfer into the middle of a block from any other block.

6.3 How to Use Blocks Effectively

If the general ideas of local and global variables have been understood, it should not be too hard now to see how to take advantage of block structures in organizing a program.

Suppose first that the goal is to conserve storage by allocating temporary variables and arrays so that some of them share locations. Proceed as follows. The complete program must, of course, be a block. Divide the complete program block into several sub-blocks, each of which will then be independent of the others. Make the division so that temporary variables and arrays in one sub-block are never needed in the others. Declare only the temporary identifiers in the sub-blocks; any information that must be common to all sub-blocks should be declared in the complete program block.

Examples of this technique that are both small and realistic are hard to find. Therefore, we shall look at one that is not completely realistic, in that one would never go to this kind of bother for such a small program, but that is otherwise fully indicative of the method and purpose.

Suppose that three formulas are to be evaluated:

$$\text{Ans1} = \frac{2}{b^2}\left(\frac{-1}{(a+bx)^{\frac{1}{2}}} + \frac{a}{3\,(a+bx)^{\frac{3}{2}}}\right)$$

$$\text{Ans2} = \frac{x\sqrt{x^2 - a^2}}{2} + \frac{a^2}{2}\ln|x + \sqrt{x^2 - a^2}|$$

$$\text{Ans3} = \sqrt{b^2 - x^2} + \frac{b^2}{\sqrt{b^2 - x^2}}$$

Values of a, b, and x are to be read; the values of a, b, x, Ans1, Ans2, and Ans3 are to be printed. The question is how to break the program into blocks so that storage space will not be wasted.

In the first formula it looks like a good idea to compute the square root of $a + bx$ once, then to cube it for the second term, since a square root

takes a lot longer than cubing. This temporary variable will need a name; let us call it *temp*. In the second formula we would similarly save time by computing $\sqrt{x^2 - a^2}$ once, and a little bit of time can be saved by computing a^2 only once. Call these temporary variables *root* and *asq*. Likewise, the third formula could make use of two variables that might be called *root* and *bsq*.

Now we should think about how to set up blocks and what should be declared in each in order to minimize storage requirements. It is clear that not all of the five temporary variables are ever needed at once, so we ought to set up blocks to use the same storage wherever possible. The simplest way to accomplish the desired result is to make the computation of each formula a separate block and to declare the temporary variables in these; the input and output variables can be declared in the "outer" block. Proceeding accordingly, we arrive at the program shown in Figure 6.4.

Despite its unrealistically small size, there is a great deal to be learned from study of this program. First, it is immaterial for our purposes so far whether the Read and Print operations are placed in the sub-blocks. The variables appearing in them are local to the main program block and global to the sub-blocks; there is no difficulty either way. Putting them in the main program block does facilitate separate compilation of the sub-blocks, however, a subject to which we shall return later.

It is worth noting that block structure accomplishes nothing in this example that could not be done without it—but with more effort. The stated goal was to conserve storage; this could also have been accomplished without sub-blocks. We could have declared two temporary variables in the heading of one main program block and used these two in the computation of each formula. In a small program like this one there would have been no great inconvenience in doing so; about the only annoyance would have been that the names could not have been as descriptive of what the variables represented at each point.

In a large program, however, this very matter of keeping the temporary variables straight becomes quite awkward. Not only would the names have to be meaningless, it would be crucial to know at all times exactly which ones were still needed. In a program with a complex pattern of statement execution it is almost impossible to be both efficient and accurate in this regard. Block structure thus makes it possible to break a large job into little pieces that are more easily managed and still produce an efficient program.

Suppose now that we were worried about computing x^2 twice (in the second and third sub-blocks) and we wanted to set up one variable name that would have the same meaning in both sub-blocks in order to compute x^2 once and then use it in both places. How could we do it? One way, of course, would be to declare a temporary variable for x^2 in the main program block, but this would in general be wasteful, since it is not needed in the first sub-block. The simple solution would be to set up one more level of blocks: place the second and third sub-blocks of the program of Figure 6.4 in another sub-block of the main program. This new block would declare the temporary variable for x^2 and would contain the present blocks for computing Ans2 and Ans3. (We emphasize once again that although no one would ever bother with these techniques in such a small program the concepts are still valid.)

Note that two of the sub-blocks declare variables named *root*. *These are not the same variable!* They have the same name, they are used for similar purposes, and an ALGOL processor might by chance assign them to the same storage location—but they are still completely independent. A variable is unknown in any block in which it is neither local nor global. If it were desired to make these

two the same variable, it would be necessary to declare it *once* in a higher level block, so that it would become global to both.

This does raise a sticky point, however. Suppose that a variable declared in one block has the same name as a variable that is global to that block. What happens? Answer: the global variable becomes unknown as long as the sub-block is being executed. The value of the global variable is not lost, but as long as control is in the sub-block the name will refer to the local variable.

This "temporary forgetting" of a variable declared in a higher level block can be used deliberately to advantage and can also cause trouble for the unwary. It can be helpful when several programmers are working on the same job and do not want to have to check that they have never used the same names for temporary variables. Another example would be a program borrowed from someone else.

On the other hand, the unintentional duplication of a variable name can lead to errors that are quite difficult to diagnose; it may therefore be worthwhile to suggest a mechanical procedure for avoiding it. We assume for now that the primary reason for using blocks is to conserve storage and to split a large job into manageable pieces. For this purpose it will often be sufficient to have only one level of block structure, as in the example under consideration. In such a situation one can stay out of trouble by following this procedure: declare in the

```
begin real a, b, x, Ans1, Ans2, Ans3;
Read (a, b, x);
        begin real temp;
        temp := sqrt (a + b × x);
        Ans1 := (2/b ↑ 2) × (−1/temp + a/(3 × temp ↑ 3))
        end;
        begin real root, asq;
        asq := a ↑ 2;
        root := sqrt (x ↑ 2 − asq);
        Ans2 := x × root/2 + (asq/2) × ln (abs (x + root))
        end;
        begin real root, bsq;
        bsq := b ↑ 2;
        root := sqrt (bsq − x ↑ 2);
        Ans3 := root + bsq/root
        end;
Print (a, b, x, Ans1, Ans2, Ans3)
end
```

Figure 6.4. A program using block structure to conserve storage.

main program block only those variables that are needed in several sub-blocks or that are needed for "communication" between sub-blocks. *Keep a list of these variables handy on a separate sheet of paper.* Every time a new temporary variable is to be declared in a sub-block, check that its name has not already been used. (There is no need to be concerned about using the same name in several sub-blocks, since with only one level of block structure all such names will be independent.) If a program requires more than one level of blocks, a slightly more complex checking system can be devised. The basic idea is always to avoid declaring a variable that has the same name as some variable that is already global to the block.

6.4   Dynamic Storage Allocation

The ALGOL block concept provides another capability that in some problems may be the difference between a relatively simple fast program and a complex slow one. It is possible to define the sizes of arrays in terms of program variables, which means that the determination of the sizes of arrays and the allocation of storage to them is not done until the program is executed (more precisely, upon entry to a block in which variable size arrays are declared). Thus, if a program involves a number of arrays, not all of which reach their maximum dimensions simultaneously, dynamic storage allocation makes it possible to employ the storage available to best advantage.

We spoke in Chapter 5 of the lower and upper *bounds* for each subscript position in an array declaration; at that time we showed all bound pairs as numbers. Actually, a subscript bound may be any arithmetic expression, with the one restriction that all variables used must be global to the block in which the array is declared. This last is for the simple reason that declarations must appear in the heading of a block, before any data has been read and before any assignment statements have been carried out; local variables could therefore not yet have been given values. There is no question of stating maximum sizes in an outer block and detailing the actual—variable—size in an inner block. In fact, this would destroy the whole scheme, since it would amount to using the same name for both a local and a global variable.

The restriction to global variables in subscript bound expressions does mean that any arrays declared in the outermost block of a program must necessarily have fixed sizes. This is in the nature of things; it could not be avoided, and there would be no way to take advantage of any scheme that might be devised to avoid it.

An example of dynamic storage allocation appears in Case Study 7, Section 6.7.

6.5   Separate Compilation

The block structure idea provides another kind of flexibility: the ability to compile a part of a program without compiling the other parts. In many situations this is more important than dynamic storage allocation.

Returning to the program of Figure 6.4, imagine that each formula is a large computation involving hundreds of statements and many days of programming. What would happen if it were necessary to have three different people do the three parts? As this program has been set up, each would be able to write and test his own part separately, with the three parts being combined into one program after the parts were completed.

This can be done as follows. After writing the program for one formula, that block can be put together with the over-all program block and compiled; all variables are defined and input and output will operate correctly (although not all results will be printed). Using a separate copy of the main program block, the programmers working on the second and third formulas can similarly compile and check out their pieces. A reshuffling of cards then puts the whole program together ready to be compiled into one complete object program.

Naturally, the procedure might not be so simple in a large job. In particular, if the three parts are not independent, as they are here, but instead depend on the results produced by the others, more elaborate things have to be done to enable the parts to be tested separately. But this is true in any case; no compiler can solve this problem without some thought on the part of the programmer.

6.6   Own Variables

We have seen that after exit from a block the values of all variables declared in the block are lost and that this is done deliberately to allow multiple storage assignments for variables that are not needed simultaneously. It can happen, however, that we may wish to preserve the value of a variable declared in a block after exit from it, when the block structure idea is being used for some other purpose than to conserve storage for such a variable.

The *own* declaration makes it possible to specify that a variable is to retain its value after leaving the block in which the declaration is made. When the block is re-entered, an own variable has the same value it had at the time of the last exit from the block, even though it remains undefined until re-entry.

This does raise some problems, however. A variable cannot be referred to when it is neither local nor global, and an own variable is neither until the first entry into the block where it is declared. Therefore, no value can be assigned to the own variable until the block where it is declared is reached. One of the statements in the block must therefore assign a value to it. This value is preserved after leaving the block. Now, what happens when the block is entered again? The value has been preserved, but the assignment statement to give it a value will again assign a value to it—and if this is done, why save its value at all? One is first tempted to suggest that an initial value be assigned to it before entering the block—but this, of course, is illegal, since the variable is neither local nor global at a point where this would have to be done.

The situation is not hopeless, however. With a moderately simple device, it is possible to avoid this apparent logical problem. We may illustrate the technique by developing a program segment to produce the next term of the Fibonacci sequence each time it is entered.

The Fibonacci sequence is 1, 1, 2, 3, 5, 8, 13, 21, etc., where each term (except the first two) is the sum of the two preceding terms. We can set up the computation of the next term as a separate block simply by saving the last two terms each time the block is entered, but some way must be devised to get the process started properly.

Let us call the two most recent terms *Fib* and *PrevFib*. Once these two variables have been made equal to 1, then a new term can always be found by the statements

$$Temp := Fib + PrevFib;$$
$$PrevFib := Fib;$$
$$Fib := Temp;$$

These statements compute the next term and reassign the values of the two most recent terms. The question is, how can we set up the assignment of the initial values to *Fib* and *PrevFib* in such a way that it will be done only once?

The program segment to do this is to be a block. Suppose that at some point in the program containing this block, which is placed to be executed only at the beginning of the program, we assign the value 1 to a variable named *which*. This variable must naturally be declared in the "outer" block so that it is global to the block that computes the next Fibonacci number. Now consider the block shown in Figure 6.5. We see that Fib and PrevFib have been declared as own variables and that a switch has been declared. Each time the block is entered, the switch will be encountered. The first time, *which* is equal to 1, and we go to the statement labeled *first*. Here we give Fib and PrevFib their starting values and set *which* equal to 2. The program then continues to compute the next number. Every time after the first the switch will cause a transfer to the statement labeled *thereafter*, thus bypassing the initialization.

The variable named *Next*, which must be global to this block, always contains the next Fibonacci

```
Fibonacci:  begin own integer Fib, PrevFib; integer Temp;
                switch S := first, thereafter;
            go to S [which];
first:      Fib := PrevFib := 1;
            which := 2;
thereafter: Temp := Fib + PrevFib;
            PrevFib := Fib;
            Next := Fib := Temp
            end
```

Figure 6.5. Program using an "own" variable in a block to compute the next Fibonacci number.

$$a_{11}x_1 \qquad\qquad\qquad = b_1$$

$$a_{21}x_1 + a_{22}x_2 \qquad\qquad = b_2$$

$$a_{31}x_1 + a_{32}x_2 + a_{33}x_3 \qquad = b_3$$

$$\cdots\cdots\cdots\cdots\cdots\cdots\cdots\cdots\cdots\cdots$$

$$a_{n1}x_1 + a_{n2}x_2 + a_{n3}x_3 + \cdots + a_{nn}x_n = b_n$$

Figure 6.6.   The system of equations to be solved in Case Study 7.

number on exit from the block. The first number generated is 2; if it were desired to generate the sequence from the start, that is, produce 1, 1, 2, 3, 5, $\cdots$, the switch arrangement could be modified to do so.

This has all the appearances of begging the question: if we can arrange to execute the statement that sets *which* to 1 only once, why cannot we arrange to set Fib and PrevFib to their initial values only once? The answer is that *Fib* and *PrevFib* are local to the block where they are declared, whereas *which* is global to it.

There are other ways to accomplish the same result without using a switch, but they must depend on some variable that is global to the block where the own variable is declared.

6.7   Case Study 7: Simultaneous Equations

We are given a system of simultaneous linear algebraic equations, as in Case Study 6, except that the matrix of coefficients is special: all elements above the main diagonal are zero. This is called a lower triangular system and is represented in Figure 6.6.

Such a system is trivial to solve, of course, by simple substitution into each equation of the variables already found. The thing that makes it interesting to us is the question of avoiding the wasting of a large amount of storage. There are two aspects to this situation. For one thing, we would like to set up a program that will handle any number of equations up to some maximum, but we would prefer not to establish the arrays as having that maximum, regardless of the number of equations in a particular set of data. This implies dynamic storage allocation. The second consideration is that if we took the obvious step of making the coefficients into a two-dimensional array, about half the array would never have anything in it.

The approach to be taken in this Case Study is to set up the coefficients in a *one*-dimensional array of variable size and to develop subscript expressions that will locate the desired elements of this array in terms of the row and column numbers of the array as written in Figure 6.6. To begin with, let us make a notational change in the array as shown to regard the constant terms as elements of the system array, each constant term being immediately to the right of the last coefficient in its row. This amounts to the notational change $a_{i,i+1} = b_i$.

It is essential that the notation be completely clear, so consider an example of a system of three equations. These would be written

$$a_{11}x_1 = a_{12}$$

$$a_{21}x_1 + a_{22}x_2 = a_{23}$$

$$a_{31}x_1 + a_{32}x_2 + a_{33}x_3 = a_{34}$$

We propose to make these coefficients and constants the elements of a one-dimensional array, in which the nine quantities in this example would be laid out like this:

$$a_{11} \quad a_{12} \quad a_{21} \quad a_{22} \quad a_{23} \quad a_{31} \quad a_{32} \quad a_{33} \quad a_{34}$$

In other words, the rows are placed in the array in succession.

The next, and most important, question is how to reference an element in this array in terms of the original row and column number of the element. We can start by searching for a general expression that would give the number of elements in the array for a system of n equations. Observe that the numbers of the elements in the rows of the original system form the series

$$2 + 3 + \cdots + (n + 1)$$

This series contains n terms; we can rewrite it as

$$(1 + 2 + \cdots + n) + n$$

The sum of the first n integers is given by $n(n + 1)/2$. By adding n to this and rearranging, we get for the total number of elements in the system $n(n + 3)/2$.

Now consider the question of locating an element in the one-dimensional array in terms of its row and column number in the original system. We may begin by deciding that the elements in the one-dimensional array will be numbered from 1. Applying a modification of the formula above, we get for the number of the last element of row

$i - 1$: $(i-1)(i-1+3)/2 = (i-1)(i+2)/2$. The first element in the ith row, therefore, has the number $(i-1)(i+2)/2+1$. This evidently must also be the number of the element in row i, column 1; it appears that the number of the element in row i column j must be: $(i-1)(i+2)/2 + j$.

Setting $j = i$, we get for the number of the diagonal element in row i: $(i-1)(i+2)/2+i$. The number of the constant term in row i is then $(i-1)(i+2)/2+i+1$, which can be rewritten as $i(i+3)/2$.

Let us summarize these formulas. Transforming a lower diagonal system of simultaneous equations into a one-dimensional array numbered from 1, with the constant term in each equation entered immediately following the last coefficient in its row, we get the following for the one-dimensional element number:

Element in row i column $j = (i-1)(i+2)/2+j$
Diagonal element in row $i = (i-1)(i+2)/2+i$
Constant term in row $i = i(i+3)/2$

The total number of elements in the array $= n(n+3)/2$

Now we should think about how to get the elements of this array into the machine. In many practical problems the system of equations would be generated by a previous section of the program, and some following section would use the results. Here, however, to make the discussion a little more coherent, we shall assume that the coefficients and constants are to be read from cards and the solution printed. The question now is how to organize the card deck to make it as simple as possible and still have some protection against card-handling errors. As usual, there are many ways to proceed. The approach chosen here is to place each element, together with its row and column number, on a separate card. As each card is read, the row and column information can be used to determine where in the array to store the value on the card. The end of the deck will be signaled by a card having a row number of zero. With this arrangement, the elements do not need to be entered in sequence, which is a convenience.

With an additional statement or two in the program, we can also arrange another convenience: zero elements need not be entered at all. This merely requires clearing the array to zeros before starting to read cards.

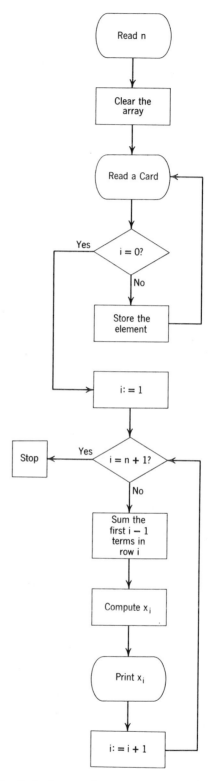

Figure 6.7. Block diagram of the method of solution of Case Study 7.

Since the size of the system to be solved is left variable, it will be necessary to place at the front of the deck a card containing the value of n, the number of equations. This must be read at the very beginning of the program, before entering the block that will do the work, because we wish to declare the variable size of the element array upon entering that block. The first part of the block diagram in Figure 6.7 shows the logic of card reading.

With the cards read and the elements entered, we are ready to start computing the values of the unknowns. This will require two for-loops, one to run through the equations in order, and a second to sum the terms in each row up to the diagonal. This involves no new concepts. The block diagramming of for-loops of this kind is a bit awkward without special diagramming notation, which we do not choose to introduce. The two loops have been represented rather differently. One is shown explicitly, in terms of the literal meaning of the for-step-until construction, and the other has been summarized by the word "sum." The diagram could naturally have been drawn in other ways, but this seems to be a reasonable compromise between an awkward complete explicitness and a hard-to-follow terseness. Some such compromise is usually necessary.

The program of Figure 6.8 merits a few comments. The block structure here is used for the sole purpose of getting variable size in the array of coefficients and constants, recalling that variables in subscript bound expressions must be global to the block where the declaration is made. The reading of the value of n, the number of equations, must be outside the inner block for this reason. (More precisely, the reading *and declaration* must be outside the inner block.)

The compound statement between **begin** and **end** after the second for-statement *is not a block*, since it contains no declarations.

The most interesting thing about this program, and about the Case Study, is the use of moderately complex subscript expressions to make a variable size one-dimensional array do what would ordinarily be set up as a two-dimensional array. The particular techniques used here are not in themselves fundamental, but the general idea of the sort of thing that can be done to conserve storage is quite important. The reader will be amply rewarded for the effort necessary to understand the workings of this program.

```
begin integer n;
Read (n);
          begin integer i, j; real element, sum;
                  real array x [1:n], a [1:n × (n + 3)/2];
              for i : = 1 step 1 until n × (n + 3)/2 do a [i] : = 0;
more data:    Read (i, j, element);
              if i = 0 then go to compute;
              a [(i − 1) × (i + 2)/2 + j] : = element;
              go to more data;
compute:      for i : = 1 step 1 until n do
                  begin
                  sum : = 0;
                  for j : = 1 step 1 until i − 1 do
                      sum : = sum + a [(i − 1) × (i + 2)/2 + j] × x [j];
                  x [i] : = (a [i × (i + 3)/2] − sum)/a [(i − 1) × (i + 2)/2 + i];
                  Print (i, x [i])
                  end
          end
end
```

Figure 6.8. Program for Case Study 7.

EXERCISES

1. Set up program segments with switch declarations to do the following.

a. If n = −2, y = 6x − c sin x
   n = −1, y = 3ax² + b + c cos x
   n =   0, y = ax³ + bx + c sin x
   n =   1, y = $\frac{ax^4}{4} + \frac{bx^2}{2} - c \cos x$

Assume that $-2 \leq n \leq 1$ and that n is an integer.

*b. If $0 \leq a \leq 9$, y = re^(x+1.117)
   $10 \leq a \leq 19$, y = se^(x+1.57)
   $20 \leq a \leq 29$, y = te^(x+2.89)
   $30 \leq a \leq 39$, y = ue^(x+3.04)

Assume $0 \leq a \leq 39$ and that a is an integer.

c. If $0.5 \leq t < 1.5$, y = a + bx + cx²
   $1.5 \leq t < 2.5$, y = (a sin bx)ᶜ
   $2.5 \leq t < 3.5$, y = $\sqrt{a + bx^3} - c$
   $3.5 \leq t < 4.5$, y = $a \ln \left| b + \frac{c}{x} \right|$

Assume $0.5 \leq t < 4.5$ and that t is real.

*d. If $1 \leq k < 2$, y = g
   $2 \leq k < 3$, y = gx
   $3 \leq k < 4$, y = gx² + h
   $4 \leq k < 5$, y = gx³ + hx + i
   $5 \leq k < 6$, y = gx⁴ + hx² + ix

Assume $1 \leq k < 6$ and that k is real.

2. Make a table similar to Table 6.1 for each of the following block structures.

```
a. A: begin real r;
   B:     begin real s;
   C:         begin real t;
              end C;
          end B;
      end A;
*b. A: begin real u;
   B:     begin real v;
          end B;
   C:     begin real w;
          end C;
   D:     begin real x;
          end D;
      end A;
*c. A: begin real g;
   B:     begin real h;
   C:     begin real i;
          end C;
   D:     begin real j;
   E:         begin real k;
              end E;
          end D;
          end B;
   F:     begin real l;
          end F;
      end A;
```

```
d. A: begin real p;
   B:     begin real q;
          end B;
   C:     begin real r;
   D:         begin real s;
   E:             begin real t;
                  end E;
   F:             begin real u;
                  end F;
              end D;
   G:         begin real v;
              end G;
          end C;
   H:     begin real w;
          end H;
      end A;
```

3. Write programs to read all variables, compute results, and print input and output for the following. Use temporary variables to conserve object program time and block structure to conserve object program storage space.

a. $r = \dfrac{-(x^2 - a^2)^{5/2}}{4x^4} + \dfrac{3(x^2 - a^2)^{3/2}}{8a^2x^2} + \dfrac{3(x^2 - a^2)^{1/2}}{8a^2}$

$s = \dfrac{x^3}{3} - \dfrac{a^3}{3} \ln |a^3 + x^3|$

$t = \dfrac{6}{ax} - 2(ax)^3 + 2 \ln |ax|$

*b. $h = \sqrt{a^2 - x^2} \ln a + \dfrac{|\ln a|}{\sqrt{a^2 - x^2 + 1}}$

$= b^2 \sqrt{a^2 - x^2} + \dfrac{3}{b^4 \sqrt{a^2 - x^2}} - \dfrac{1}{b^2} \arctan \dfrac{x}{a}$

$j = \dfrac{(x^2 + a^2)^{5/2}}{5} - \dfrac{2c^2(x^2 + a^2)^{3/2}}{3} + c^4(x^2 + a^2)^{1/2}$

$k = \dfrac{-x^6}{(x^2 + a^2)^{1/2}} - \dfrac{x^3}{3(x^2 + a^2)^{3/2}}$

$\quad + \ln(x + \sqrt{x^2 + a^2})$

c. $f = \dfrac{\ln a}{(x^2 + b^2)^{1/2}} + \dfrac{x^2(1 + b)}{\ln a} + \dfrac{1}{x}$

$g = \sin(a + x) + \dfrac{\sin^2(a + x)}{3b}$

$h = \dfrac{e^x}{\sqrt{x^2 + a^2}} - \sqrt{1 + e^x}$

$i = e^{\sqrt{x}} \sqrt{\sqrt{x} + \sqrt{x^2 + a^2}}$

$j = \sqrt{x^2 + a^2} \arctan \dfrac{x}{a} - \dfrac{\ln b}{\arctan \dfrac{x}{a}}$

*d. $p = a\sqrt{a^2 + x^2} + \dfrac{b}{\sqrt{a^2 + x^2}}$

$q = a^2(a^2 + x^2)^{3/2} - b^2(a^2 + x^2)^{1/2} + \dfrac{ab}{(a^2 + x^2)^{1/2}}$

$r = a \ln(a - x) + b(a - x)^3$

$s = a^3b^2(a - x)^{1/3}$

4. Exercises 1k–1m of Chapter 5 provide a method of sorting the elements of a one-dimensional array into ascending or descending sequence. Given two one-dimensional arrays of 20 elements each, named *a* and *b*, print the elements of each in ascending sequence *without disturbing the original arrays*. (Block structure is not really needed here, since the same temporary array could be used in doing both sorts, but do it anyway for practice.)

5. An upper triangular system of simultaneous equations is one in which all elements below the main diagonal are zero. Given the same card input arrangement as in Case Study 7, write a program to solve such a system along the lines of Case Study 7.

7. PROCEDURES

7.1 Introduction

It fairly often happens that some basic computation is required at a number of places in a program. It is possible, of course, to write out the necessary statements each time they are needed, but doing so wastes programmer time and machine storage space and is conducive to errors. It would seem desirable to be able to write the statements *once* and then to refer to them whenever the computation is needed. *Procedures* provide this capability.

It also frequently happens that many programmers have need of some common computation, such as square root or cosine; it would be unreasonable for everyone to have to write a routine to do these widely used operations. Instead, they are set up as procedures that can be incorporated into an object program by the processor and are called into action simply by writing their names. (We shall see below that these particular procedures are somewhat special in that they do not require a *procedure declaration*.) Even when a procedure is not included in the list of those available automatically, it still happens that one programmer would like to be able to borrow something written by another and incorporate it into his program with a minimum of effort. This is valuable, even though the procedure may be called into action only once. Here, we are interested in the saving of programming time instead of the saving of storage space.

For whatever reason, it is most convenient to be able to set up a group of statements in one place in a program and to refer to them as needed.

7.2 The Procedure Heading and Procedure Body

We must distinguish carefully between the *definition* of the processing to be done by a procedure and the *use* of that procedure. We define a procedure with a *procedure declaration*, which consists of a *procedure heading* and a *procedure body*. The procedure heading gives the name of the procedure, together with (usually) the names of the parameters of the procedure and certain information about them. The procedure body consists of a statement, a compound statement, or, most commonly, a block.

Let us consider an extremely elementary example. Suppose that in a certain program it is frequently necessary to compute one of the roots of the quadratic equation

$$ax^2 + bx + c = 0,$$

given values of a, b, and c. A procedure to do this can be defined as follows:

procedure root (a, b, c, x);

   x := $(-b + \mathrm{sqrt}\,(b \uparrow 2 - 4 \times a \times c))/$

                          $(2 \times a);$

(We assume, for our purposes here, that this statement is valid, that is, the root is real and a is not zero.)

This declaration defines a procedure to carry out certain processing. Its appearance in a program would cause a group of machine instructions to be inserted in the object program, but it would not by itself cause any processing to take place. That occurs as a result of *calling* the procedure, which is done by writing its name with *actual parameters* in place of the *formal parameters* in the declaration.

Suppose now that it is desired to compute one of the roots of a quadratic equation in which the coefficient of x^2 is 16.9, the coefficient of x is $r - s$, the constant term is $T + 12$, and the root is to be stored as the new value of a variable named *answer*. All this is done by writing the procedure call:

root (16.9, r − s, T + 12, answer);

The call will cause the formal parameters a, b, c, and x to be replaced by the actual parameters 16.9, $r - s$, $T + 12$, and *answer*, just as though the procedure body had been written

$$\text{answer} := (-(r - s) + \text{sqrt} ((r - s) \uparrow 2 - 4 \times (16.9) \times (T + 12)))/(2 \times 16.9);$$

If at some other place we want one root of the equation $x^2 - 7x + \log (2 + g) = 0$, with the root called *result*, we could write the procedure call

root (1.0, −7.0, ln (2 + g), result);

For a particularly instructive example, suppose we wanted the root of the equation $2x^2 + ax + b = 0$, with the result to be called *xvalue*. The procedure call would be

root (2, a, b, xvalue);

The crucial concept is that the actual parameters a and b in this call have nothing to do with the formal parameters a and b in the procedure declaration. The formal parameters are no more than dummy variables that indicate what to do with the actual parameters in the call; the actual param-

eters are expressions involving actual variables that have been declared elsewhere in the program that calls the procedure. In this example the formal parameter a would be replaced in the body by 2, the formal parameter b by a, the formal parameter c by b, and the formal parameter x by *xvalue*. Usually a procedure body is a block because it will have local variables; if the names of any actual parameters are the same as the names of local variables in the body, the latter will be changed when the procedure is called.

For an example of a procedure having as its body a compound statement, suppose we wanted *both* roots of the quadratic equation. The procedure declaration could be

procedure root2 (a, b, c, x1, x2);
begin
x1 := (−b + sqrt (b ↑ 2 − 4 × a × c))/(2 × a);
x2 := (−b − sqrt (b ↑ 2 − 4 × a × c))/(2 × a)
end

This example shows how it is usually desirable to make a procedure body a block: there is really no point in computing the square root twice—better to give it a name and compute it once. But to give it a name requires a declaration of the name, which in turn requires a block.

> **procedure** root2 (a, b, c, x1, x2);
> **begin real** temp;
> temp := sqrt (b ↑ 2 − 4 × a × c);
> x1 := (−b + temp)/(2 × a);
> x2 := (−b − temp)/(2 × a)
> **end**

Consider an example in which one of the input parameters is an array and in which there are two output variables. Suppose that in a certain program it is frequently necessary to find the largest element (in absolute value) in a specified row of an $n \times n$ array. The input to the procedure is

procedure big element (a, i, n, aij, j);
begin
integer k;
aij := abs (a [i, l]);
j := 1;
for k := 2 **step** 1 **until** n **do**
    if abs (a [i, k]) > aij **then begin** aij := a [i, k]; j := k **end**
end

Figure 7.1. Procedure to find the largest element in a specified row of an array.

therefore the name of the array, the row number, and n. The output is to be the largest element in the row and its column number.

While we are about it, let us introduce another way of writing the parameters in a procedure declaration or procedure call. So far, we have used the comma as the *delimiter* between parameters. It is also possible to substitute the following for the comma:

> a *right* parenthesis, followed by
> a string of letters, followed by
> a colon, followed by
> a *left* parenthesis

Thus, in this example, we will have a procedure heading something like

> **procedure** big element (a, i, n, aij, j) ;

where a is the name of the array, i the row number, n the order of the array, aij the largest element, and j its column number. To make the declaration more readable, we may write

> **procedure** big element (a) row: (i) order:
> (n) element: (aij) column: (j) ;

This variation is available if and where we may wish to use it. It has no effect on the operation of the program; it may be used in the declaration and not in the call, or vice versa. Used with discretion, it can help to make a program more understandable to someone else. Note that this substitution applies only to the *commas* in a parameter list. There is no way to give a description of the *first* parameter and therefore no way to use this facility in a procedure having only one parameter.

The program shown in Figure 7.1 presents no great difficulties. We start by assigning the first element of the given row as the assumed largest and then compare it with each of the other elements in the row. Any time a larger element is found, it becomes the largest and its column number is assigned to the output column number. When all elements in the row have been tested in this way, aij will contain the largest element in absolute value and j will contain its column number.

With this declaration in the heading of some block, suppose now that we want the largest element in the third row of a 19 x 19 array called *chi matrix*, this largest to be assigned to the variable named *biggest* and its column number to *column*. We write the statement

big element (chi matrix, 3, 19, biggest, column) ;

or

> big element (chi matrix) row: (3) order:
> (19) element: (biggest) column: (column) ;

7.3 Functions

The procedure calls we have seen so far have been complete statements in themselves. When such a procedure call is encountered in the execution of the program, it brings the procedure body into action and does whatever processing is specified (usually including assignment of new values to actual parameters). Control then passes on to the statement following the procedure call.

When only one variable is assigned a new value as the result of executing a procedure, the procedure call can be considerably simplified by making the procedure a *function*. When this is done, writing the name of the procedure calls it into action, as before, but now the name itself represents a value that is used where the procedure name is written. In other words, the procedure represents a variable with the same name.

A procedure is made into a function by preceding the word **procedure** with a type (real, integer, or Boolean) and assigning a value to the procedure within the procedure body. For instance, suppose we wanted to make the calculation of one root of the quadratic a function:

real procedure root1 (a, b, c);
root1 := ($-$b + sqrt (b$\uparrow$2 $-$ 4 $\times$ a $\times$ c)/(2 $\times$ a);

Now, if we want to get one root of the quadratic $3x^2 - fx - 12 = 0$, add it to a variable named *theta*, and assign the sum as the new value of a variable named *kappa*, we can write simply

> kappa := theta + root1 (3.0, $-$f, $-$12.0);

Or suppose we wanted to get one root of the equation $(a - 8)x^2 + x - \cos w = 0$, square it, subtract the natural logarithm of z, and assign all this as the new value of q:

> q := root1 (a $-$ 8, 1.0, $-\cos$ (w)) $\uparrow$ 2 $-$ ln (z);

In short, a function is used by writing its name wherever its value is desired in any place that a variable may be used. It is defined in the same way a procedure is defined, with a type before the

```
begin real temp1, temp2, temp3, a, b, n, sum4, sum2, h, x, K, Percenteff;
real procedure E (x);
E : = 1/(x ↑ 5 × (exp (1.432/(K × x)) − 1));
Read (temp1, temp2, temp3, a, b, n);
h : = (b − a)/n;
for K : = temp1 step temp2 until temp3 do
    begin
    sum4 : = sum2 : = 0.0;
    for x : = a + h step 2 × h until b − 3 × h do
        begin
        sum4 : = sum4 + E (x);
        sum2 : = sum2 + E (x + h)
        end;
    Percenteff : = 64.77 × h/3 × (4 × sum4 + 2 × sum2 + E(a) + 4 × E (b − h) + E (b))/K ↑ 4;
    Print (K, Percenteff)
    end
end
```

Figure 7.2. Luminous efficiency program of Case Study 4, written with a function.

word **procedure** and with an assignment statement to give a value to the function.

When this is done, the name of the procedure (function) is *not* local to the procedure body. The name must not be declared within the body, and the name must never appear anywhere but on the left-hand side of an assignment statement. This avoids confusion with recursive procedures, discussed in Section 7.7.

For another example of a function, consider the evaluation of Planck's equation that we met in Case Study 4, Section 4.4. Omitting the constant multiplier, which was handled separately there, the formula was

$$E = \frac{1}{x^5 \left(e^{\frac{1.432}{Kx}} - 1 \right)}$$

This is easily set up as a function:

```
real procedure E(x);
E : = 1/(x ↑ 5 × (exp (1.432/(K × x)) − 1));
```

The value of Planck's formula, given K and x, may be used in an expression simply by writing the name followed by parentheses enclosing the actual argument. The program for the case study is now much simpler, as shown in Figure 7.2.

Note that K is neither a formal parameter nor local to the procedure body (which is not even a block, of course). Therefore, it must be global

to the procedure body. There is nothing to prevent this. As a matter of fact, it is permissible to have nothing but global variables, that is, no formal (or actual) parameters.

It happens that x is used as a formal parameter in the procedure declaration and in some cases as an actual parameter in the function call. This also is legal, but always remember that the two are unrelated. The formal parameter x indicates what to do with the actual parameter when the function is called; it has no value and is never declared. The actual parameter x is the name of a variable that has been declared elsewhere in the program; the fact that it has the same name as the formal parameter is a coincidence that has no bearing on how the procedure body is executed.

7.4 Call by Name and Call by Value

It is worth emphasizing exactly what happens to the actual parameters when a procedure is called. The idea is illustrated in the following example, which at the same time suggests a little of the range and power of procedures.*

Suppose we need to compute the following three sums.

* The example is similar to one in Bottenbruch, "Structure and Use of ALGOL 60," *Journal of the Association for Computing Machinery*, Volume 9, Number 2 (April 1962).

$$e = \sum_{x=1}^{20} x^2$$

$$f = \sum_{y=3}^{14} \cos (0.1 \times y)$$

$$g = \sum_{t=0}^{8} (a + z1[t] + z2[t])^{\frac{1}{2}}$$

Different as these may appear, they can be handled by one procedure in a rather simple manner. We shall set up a procedure to handle a general summation of the form

$$s = \sum_{i=m}^{n} f$$

where we understand that f, the function being summed, involves the index of summation i.

This is easily set up as a procedure.

```
procedure sum (s, i, m, n, f);
begin
s : = 0;
for i : = m step 1 until n do s : = s + f
end
```

The three summations will be performed as a result of the following three procedure calls:

sum (e, x, 1, 20, x ↑ 2);

sum (f, y, 3, 14, cos (0.1 × y));

sum (g, t, 0, 8, sqrt (a + z1 [t] + z2 [t]));

The result of these three calls will be the same as the result of executing the following three compound statements:

```
begin
e : = 0;
for x : = 1 step 1 until 20 do e : = e + x ↑ 2
end;
begin
f : = 0;
for y : = 3 step 1 until 14 do f : = f + cos (0.1 × y)
end;
begin
g : = 0;
for t : = 0 step 1 until 8 do g : = g + sqrt (a + z1 [t]
    + z2 [t])
end
```

Thus we see that what is transmitted to the procedure body by a procedure call is a rule for computing values, not the values themselves. Still,

the object program machine instructions corresponding to the procedure body are in computer storage in only one place; there need not be a copy for each procedure call.

We see in this example, incidentally, that the actual parameters of a procedure call can include other procedures. (Cosine and square root are procedures, although of a "built-in" variety that does not require declarations.) In fact, we shall see in Section 7.7 that the call of a procedure may even involve that same procedure.

Let us consider another example to see how we might prefer to transmit the *value* of an expression to a procedure instead of the expression itself. Suppose we wanted to use the procedure named sum to compute the sum

$$h = \sum_{i=n+1}^{[n(n-1)]/2} i^3$$

When we write the procedure call sum (h, i, n + 1, n × (n − 1)/2, i ↑ 3);, the procedure body will in effect be changed to

```
begin
h : = 0;
for i : = n + 1 step 1 until n × (n − 1)/2 do
    h : = h + i ↑ 3
end
```

Because in the full generality of the for-statement it is possible that the expression after the **until** could change, it will be evaluated every time it is tested. Yet in this program it never will change, since it does not depend on the index of summation or on anything in the controlled statement. We would be perfectly content to have the expression evaluated once upon entry into the procedure body and to use that value in all tests.

This is precisely what happens when a parameter is *called by value*, which we indicate by writing the word **value** immediately after the formal parameter list in the declaration, followed by the names of all variables to be called by value. The procedure declaration for our example could be as follows, where we have dictated that both limits of summation should be called by value.

```
procedure sum (s, i, m, n, f); value m, n;
begin
s : = 0;
for i : = m step 1 until n do s : = s + f
end
```

Now, when the procedure is called, the expressions that are the actual parameters corresponding to the formal parameters m and n will be evaluated once at the outset and those values used throughout (although in general they could be changed in the body of the procedure).

Why not call everything by value? For one thing, the whole idea applies only to input parameters: it makes no sense to talk about finding the value of an output parameter at the outset. Second, there are several types of parameters that do not represent numerical or Boolean values: procedures, functions, labels, switches, and strings, for instance. Finally, there is a processor consideration. In programs compiled by some processors there might not be any saving in calling an actual parameter that is a *single* number or variable by value; in others there might be considerable advantage.

Calling by value is primarily a question of object program efficiency, although rare occasions may arise in which the operation of the procedure is ambiguous without it. We ignore these occasions as being quite unlikely in the vast majority of typical programs. For the sake of efficiency, we suggest the following routine approach: call by value any input parameter that actually does represent only a value.

7.5 Specifications

Nothing that we have done so far gives the processor any information about the kinds of things represented by the formal parameters—they could be real, integer, or Boolean variables; they could be strings of letters and digits; they could be switches; they could be labels; they could be procedures. The difficulty is that the object program produced from the procedure body will in general be different for different kinds of parameters, and the processor has no way of knowing what each parameter is until it translates the various procedures calls. This leads to considerable difficulty in translating the procedure and in many cases to an inefficient object program.

For a simple example of the latter, suppose that two of the formal parameters in a procedure declaration are p and q and that within the procedure body we have the expression $p \uparrow q$. What kind of object program segment should be set up to evaluate them? If q is a real variable, the object program should use the formula $p \uparrow q = e^{q \times \ln p}$, but if

q is an integer variable it should multiply p by itself q times. Since q could be either, the object program must be able to accept either, and if both actually occur the object program must handle them differently.

In most cases we do not really want this kind of generality; in this example, we would know perfectly well whether q is real or integer. Therefore, why not provide the processor with this information in the procedure declaration? This is precisely what *specifiers* allow. A specifier may be any of the following: **label, switch, string, real, integer, Boolean, procedure, real procedure, integer procedure, Boolean procedure, array, real array, integer array,** or **Boolean array.** Specifiers are written following the value list (if any). They are analogous to declarations, in a way, in that they specify certain things about the formal parameters; they are quite different from declarations in that they do not of themselves cause any action to take place, such as the assignment of storage locations to variables and arrays.

A specifier does this: it tells the processor what kind of thing to expect when actual parameters are written in procedure calls. This simplifies setting up the object program corresponding to the procedure body and removes the possibility of certain ambiguities that can arise.

Omission of specifiers often leads to completely pointless generality and to much additional work for the processor. Some ALGOL systems *require* specifiers.

Examples of specifiers appear in the case studies.

7.6 Machine Code in Procedure Bodies

ALGOL permits the body of a procedure to be written in actual machine language, or something close to it, either to do things that are impossible or inconvenient in ALGOL language or that are so commonly used that object program efficiency dictates a carefully written machine code.

All the standard functions (square root, absolute value, etc.) listed on page 19 would ordinarily be written in machine code, as would input and output procedures. Machine code procedures can be set up either as functions or as ordinary procedures. The standard functions, as we have seen, are set up as functions: writing the name and some expression for a parameter produces a value that may be used where the function name is written. Input and output operations, on the other hand, would tend to be written as procedures: writing the procedure name with parameters causes the input or output action to take place, with no value being associated with the procedure name.

Machine code functions and procedures will tend to be different at different computer installations. Each installation will have its own needs for special functions, and input-output may be different for different machines or different installations. Input and output procedures are discussed a little more fully in Chapter 8.

7.7 Recursive Procedures and Calls

ALGOL permits a procedure body to make use of itself and also permits the call of a procedure to name the procedure. Let us illustrate each of these briefly.

A procedure is to be set up to evaluate the factorial of an integer n. This can be done with a for-statement, but here we shall employ a recursive procedure body to illustrate the concept. The procedure is quite short but not exactly obvious at first glance:

real procedure factorial (n);
if n = 1 **then** factorial : = 1 **else**
    factorial : = n × factorial (n − 1);

We see that the procedure body calls the same procedure if n is not 1. If n is 2, the body says that the factorial is $2 \times$ factorial (1), which is just 2×1. Thus the procedure would be called n times to compute the factorial of n.

This is not a very good way to compute a factorial, since it is much slower than a simple two-statement computation based on a for-loop. In fact, it is rather difficult to find simple examples that show this technique to good advantage. The best examples, unfortunately for us, seem to be in things like theorem proving, language translation, and ALGOL processors. In these cases the idea of a recursive procedure is basic to the whole operation—but it would be out of the question for us

to try to delve into such applications in a book of this type.

Recursive function calls are another matter. Suppose we have to evaluate the double sum

$$d = \sum_{j=1}^{8} \sum_{k=2}^{11} (j^2 + k^2)^{\frac{1}{2}}$$

Suppose now that we have a *function* similar to the *procedure* of Section 7.4, that is, the value of the summation is assigned to *sum:*

real procedure sum (i, m, n, f);
begin real temp;
temp : = 0;
for i : = m **step** 1 **until** n **do** temp : = temp + f;
sum : = temp
end

Now, the double summation is easily written as a recursive call of the function sum:

d : = sum (j, 1, 8, sum (k, 2, 11,

                sqrt (j ↑ 2 + k ↑ 2)));

We see that the summand in the main procedure (function) call is another call of the first procedure. This does precisely what we want in evaluating the double sum.

It should be understood that the processor can still set up the object program to contain the procedure body *only once*. How this can be done is a fascinating question but unfortunately not relevant here.

Recursive procedure bodies and recursive procedure calls are potentially among the most significant features of the ALGOL language. Nevertheless, they do pose some serious problems for the writers of processors. Several of the presently available versions of ALGOL do not permit them.

7.8 Case Study 8: Special Functions

We are required to evaluate the following three formulas for fixed values of a, b, and c and a range of values of r, s, and t.

$$w = a \sinh (\pi r + bs) + ce^{(\arcsin r - \operatorname{arctanh} r/2)}$$

$$x = b^2 J_0(t/\pi) - r \sinh (b \operatorname{arctanh} r/\pi)$$

$$y = \frac{(\sqrt{c} - J_1(t)) \cos (\arcsin (1 - r^2/s)) + \ln|J_2(\pi t + s/t)|}{\arcsin \dfrac{rs}{2\pi}}$$

r: 0(0.1)1
s: 2(0.5)5
t: 1(1)10

```
real procedure sinh (x); real x;
    begin real temp;
    temp : = exp (x);
    sinh : = (temp − 1/temp)/2
    end;
real procedure arcsin (x); real x;
    arcsin : = arctan (x/sqrt (1 − x ↑ 2));
real procedure arctanh (x); real x;
    arctanh : = 0.5 ln ((1 + x)/(1 − x));
```

Figure 7.3. ALGOL procedure declarations for functions to compute a hyperbolic sine, inverse sine, and inverse hyperbolic tangent.

This example is obviously contrived and perhaps not wholly realistic. The intention is to show how a programmer can make use of ALGOL functions (procedures) in an uncomplicated way to simplify the work of programming. Things of this general nature are not uncommon.

The problem to be solved in programming this job is the occurrence of mathematical functions that are not included in the standard ALGOL set. Furthermore, every such function appears at least twice, and we would like not to have to write out the steps to evaluate these mathematical functions every time they are needed.

The first step is to express the unfamiliar functions in terms of things we can readily compute. The following identities do what we need:

Hyperbolic sine: $\sinh (x) = \dfrac{e^x - e^{-x}}{2}$

Inverse sine: $\arcsin (x) = \arctan \dfrac{x}{\sqrt{1 - x^2}}$

Inverse hyperbolic tangent:

$$\text{arctanh} (x) = \frac{1}{2} \log \frac{1 + x}{1 - x}$$

Bessel function of the first kind, integral order n:

$$J_n(x) = \frac{(x/2)^n}{n!} \left[1 - \frac{(x/2)^2}{1 \cdot (n + 1)} \right.$$
$$+ \frac{(x/2)^4}{1 \cdot 2 \, (n + 1)(n + 2)}$$
$$\left. - \frac{(x/2)^6}{1 \cdot 2 \cdot 3 \, (n + 1)(n + 2)(n + 3)} + - \cdots \right]$$

Taking these in order, an ALGOL function to compute the hyperbolic sine presents no great problems. To save computing the exponential twice, however, it would be a good idea to rewrite the

formula as

$$\sinh (x) = \frac{e^x - 1/e^x}{2}$$

The inverse sine and inverse hyperbolic tangent present no problems either. The procedure declarations for the first three functions are shown in Figure 7.3. Note that x is specified in each case as real.

The Bessel function is a little more work, since it involves the evaluation of a series and since we choose to set it up to be valid for any integer value of n. Let us look at the series first. Probably the best way to evaluate it, for our purposes here, is to derive each term from the preceding one. The exact method of doing this can be read from the algorithm in Figure 7.4 as easily as it could be described in words. The program has been set up to stop computing terms after finding one that is less than 10^{-6} times the sum so far. After the sum of the (truncated) series has been found, we compute the factorial of n and perform the calculation of the Bessel function. Note that if $n = 0$ we must be sure that the factorial of zero is correctly computed as 1, which it is in the method of Figure 7.4. Note also that x is called by value to avoid several computations of the expression that might be written as an actual parameter.

With these functions out of the way, it is relatively simple to write the main program, which is shown in Figure 7.5. It is understood that the four procedure declarations would appear in the head of this program block.

7.9   Case Study 9: An Ordinary Differential Equation

We are required to set up a procedure to integrate any differential equation of the form

$$\frac{dv}{dx} = y' = f (x, y), \qquad y = y_0 \text{ when } x = x_0$$

We choose, more or less arbitrarily, to solve this problem with one version of the Runge-Kutta method.

As in any numerical attack on an ordinary differential equation, we begin at a known point on the curve and use the equation for the derivative to locate an adjacent point. Stating the problem a little more precisely, we are given y_0 at x_0; we are

```
real procedure Bessel (x, n); value x; real x; integer n;
begin real sum, term, denom1, denom2, nfact, m;
sum : = term : = denom1 : = 1;
denom2 : = n + 1;
A:   term : = −term × (x/2) ↑ 2/(denom1 × denom2);
sum : = sum + term;
if term < 10−6 × sum then go to B;
denom1 : = denom1 + 1;
denom2 : = denom2 + 1;
go to A;
B: nfact : = 1;
for m : = 1 step 1 until n do nfact : = m × nfact;
Bessel : = (x/2) ↑ n/nfact × sum
end
```

Figure 7.4. ALGOL procedure declaration for a function to compute a Bessel function of the first kind, integral order *n*.

to find y at $x = x_0 + h, x_0 + 2h, x + 3h, \cdots$, where h is a constant interval on the x-axis. Let us say, in general terms, that we know $y = y_j$ at a point $x = x_j$; we are required to find $y = y_{j+1}$ at a point $x = x_{j+1} = x_j + h$. With the Runge-Kutta method, we find y_{j+1} by applying the following formulas in succession:

$$k_1 = h \cdot f (x_j, y_j)$$

$$k_2 = h \cdot f (x_j + h/2, y_j + k_1/2)$$

$$k_3 = h \cdot f (x_j + h/2, y_j + k_2/2)$$

$$k_4 = h \cdot f (x_j + h, y_j + k_3)$$

$$y_{j+1} = y_j + \tfrac{1}{6} (k_1 + 2k_2 + 2k_3 + k_4)$$

The procedure to carry out this computation must be able to accept four parameters: x, y, h,

and the function of x and y that gives the derivative, that is, the differential equation. We shall assume that the procedure is called once for each pair of values of x and y; in other words, the incrementing of x and the use of the values of y are handled by the calling program. The procedure shown in Figure 7.6 has been given the name RK.

Note that f is specified as a procedure; this will be the function of x and y that gives the derivative, that is, the equation to be integrated. This procedure is therefore able to integrate any differential equation once we write a function to tell it what the equation is.

Suppose we want to integrate

$$y' = \left(\frac{x^3}{5} + \frac{y^2}{2}\right)^{\!\frac{1}{3}} + 1.63\, e^{-(x+y)}$$

```
begin real a, b, c, r, s, t, pi;
(The procedure declarations of Figures 7.3 and 7.4 would be
written here)
pi : = 3.1415927;
Read (a, b, c);
for r : = 0 step 0.1 until 1 do
for s : = 2 step 0.5 until 5 do
for t : = 1 step 1 until 10 do
begin
w : = a × sinh (pi × r + b × s) + c × exp (arcsin (r) −arctanh (r/2));
x : = b ↑ 2 × Bessel (t/pi, 0) − r × sinh (b × arctanh (r/pi));
y : = ((sqrt (c) − Bessel (t, 1)) × cos (arcsin (1 − r ↑ 2/s))
      + ln (abs (Bessel (pi × t + s/t, 2))))/arcsin (r × s/(2 × pi));
Print (r, s, t, w, x, y)
end
```

Figure 7.5. Program for Case Study 8.

```
procedure RK (x, y, h, f); value x, h;
    real procedure f;
begin real k1, k2, k3, k4;
k1 := h × f (x, y);
k2 := h × f (x + h/2, y + k1/2);
k3 := h × f (x + h/2, y + k2/2);
k4 := h × f (x + h, y + k3);
y := y + (k1 + 2 × k2 + 2 × k3 + k4)/6
end
```

Figure 7.6. A procedure declaration for integration of a differential equation by the Runge-Kutta method.

Figure 7.7 is a program to do this, calling RK for the integration. The program has been set up to read from a card the initial values of x and y, the interval h, and the final value of x. The stepping of x and the printing of x-y pairs is set up as a for-loop.

Let us investigate a little more closely what happens when the program of Figure 7.7 is executed. The procedure declaration in its heading causes no computation to take place; it merely defines the function. When the procedure call RK (x, y, h, deriv) is encountered, the Runge-Kutta integration procedure is called, with the current value of x, the interval h, and the function identifier *deriv* as input parameters; y is the single output parameter. The procedure RK in turn calls the function *deriv* to evaluate the formula for the derivative at four points as required in this version of the Runge-Kutta method. With the new value of y computed for $x = x + h$, control returns to the calling program, where the new value of x and the new value of y are printed. Note the expression in the output procedure call.

We may note the three different ways x and y are used as identifiers in this example: as formal

parameters of the function *deriv*, as formal parameters of the procedure RK, and as variables in the main program, where they become actual parameters in the call of RK. Different names could have been used in each of these three places, with absolutely no effect on the operation of the complete program. On the other hand, the duplication causes no trouble to the processor or the object program and makes the source program a lot easier for us to follow.

What was gained here by setting up the integration as a procedure? Actually, not much, in this example; but suppose the integration method were much more complex and that the procedure had already been written by someone else. Now, to integrate an equation would merely require writing the calling program (with a function declaration to define the equation) and inserting the RK procedure in our program. Here we see one of the major applications of the idea of procedures: a general program, set up as a procedure, can be borrowed by other programmers, often at a great saving in effort.

EXERCISES

*1. Declare a function to compute

$$\text{denom (x)} = x^2 + \sqrt{1 + 2x + 3x^2}$$

Then write assignment statements using this function to compute

$$\text{alpha} = \frac{6.9 + y}{y^2 + \sqrt{1 + 2y + 3y^2}}$$

$$\text{beta} = \frac{2.1z + z^4}{z^2 + \sqrt{1 + 2z + 3z^2}}$$

$$\text{gamma} = \frac{\sin y}{y^4 + \sqrt{1 + 2y^2 + 3y^4}}$$

$$\text{delta} = \frac{1}{\sin^2 y + \sqrt{1 + 2 \sin y + 3 \sin^2 y}}$$

2. Declare a function to compute

$$\text{Slg (a)} = 2.549 \log \left(a + a^2 + \frac{1}{a}\right)$$

Then use the function in assignment statements to compute

$$R = X + \log X + 2.549 \log \left(X + X^2 + \frac{1}{X}\right)$$

$$S = \cos X + 2.549 \log \left(1 + X + (1 + X)^2 + \frac{1}{1 + X}\right)$$

$$T = 2.549 \log \left((A - B)^3 + (A - B)^6 + \frac{1}{(A - B)^3}\right)$$

$$U = (B[i] + 6)^2 + 2.549 \log \left(\frac{1}{B[i]} + \frac{1}{B[i]^2} + B[i]\right)$$

```
begin real x, y, h, xfirst, xfinal;
real procedure deriv (x, y);
deriv := (x ↑ 3/5 + y ↑ 2/2) ↑ (1/3)
        + 1.63 × exp (−x − y);
Read (xfirst, h, xlast, y);
for x := xfirst step h until xlast − h do
    begin
    RK (x, y, h, deriv);
    Print (x + h, y)
    end
end
```

Figure 7.7. Program to integrate a differential equation, using the function of Figure 7.6.

*3. Declare a function to compute

$$S34 (x, a) = \sqrt{x^2 - a^2}$$

Then use it in computing

$$SFK = \frac{V \cdot \sqrt{V^2 - R^2}}{2} - \frac{R^2}{2} \log |V + \sqrt{V^2 - R^2}|$$

$$PSB = \frac{(X[i]^2 - B^2)^{7/2}}{7} + \frac{2B^2 (X[i]^2 - B^2)^{5/2}}{5}$$

$$+ \frac{B^4 (X(i)^2 - B^2)^{3/2}}{3}$$

4. Declare a function to compute

$$squad (a, b, c, x) = \sqrt{ax^2 + bx + c}$$

Then use it in computing

$$ETX = \frac{4PZ + 2Q}{(4PR - Q^2)\sqrt{PZ^2 + QZ + R}}$$

$$AVP = \sqrt{RY^2 + SY + \sqrt{DY^2 + EY + 16}}$$

*5. Declare a function to compute

$$Y(x) = \begin{cases} 1 + \sqrt{1 + x^2} & \text{if } x < 0 \\ 0 & \text{if } x = 0 \\ 1 - \sqrt{1 + x^2} & \text{if } x > 0 \end{cases}$$

Then write statements to compute the following formulas, which use the mathematical function notation: "Y as a function of $a + z$," etc.

$$F = 2 + Y(a + z)$$

$$G = \frac{Y(x[k]) + Y(x[k + 1])}{2}$$

$$H = Y(\cos(2\pi x)) + 1 + Y(2\pi x)$$

6. Declare a function to compute

$$Rho (a, B, n) = \frac{a}{2\pi} \sum_{i=1}^{n} B_i$$

where B is a one-dimensional array of 50 elements and $n \leq 50$. Then use it to compute $1/2\pi$ times the sum of the first 18 elements of an array named A; call the result Some.

*7. If A is any two-dimensional array with 20 rows and 20 columns, declare a function to get the sum of the absolute values of the elements in the kth row of A, except for $a[k, k]$, that is,

$$sumnr (A, k) = \sum_{j \neq k} |A_{kj}|$$

8. A is any 20 x 20 array. Declare a function to compute

$$PD (A, i, j)$$

$$= \frac{A[i - 1, j] + A[i + 1, j] + A[i, j - 1] + A[i, j + 1]}{4}$$

Then use it to compute

$$B_{ij} = (1 - alpha) \cdot B_{ij}$$
$$+ alpha \frac{B_{i-1,j} + B_{i+1,j} + B_{i,j-1} + B_{i,j+1}}{4}$$

*9. A is a one-dimensional array with a maximum of 50 elements. Declare a procedure to compute the average of the first N elements and a count of the number of these elements that are zero. Name the procedure Avernz $(A, N, average, NZ)$.

Then use the procedure to get the average of the first 20 elements of an array named Zeta, place the average in Zmean, and place the count of zero elements in Nzcnt.

10. Same as Exercise 9, except that there is to be a fifth parameter named *error*, with the procedure parameter list to be written $A, N, average, NZ, error$. If all of the first N elements of the array are zero, set error = **true**; otherwise, set error = **false**.

11. Given a one-dimensional array with N elements, declare a procedure to compute the mean and variance of the elements, with the declaration beginning *statistics* $(A, N, mean, variance)$. The necessary definitions are

$$mean = \frac{1}{n} \sum_{i=1}^{n} A_i \qquad variance = \frac{1}{n} \sum_{i=1}^{n} A_i^2 - mean^2$$

8. INPUT AND OUTPUT

8.1 Introduction

We have chosen in this book to minimize the topic of input and output in order to concentrate on the more important (to the beginner) concept of an algorithm and how algorithms can be expressed in the ALGOL language. It should be realized, however, that in actual computer applications of any reasonable size the question of input and output becomes a major issue. Without trying to give an exhaustive treatment, we can indicate some of the typical techniques.

As a matter of fact, the extremely simplified Read and Print procedure calls that have been used so far *could* be implemented —that is, a processor could rather easily be designed to turn out usable object programs, given no more information than the names of the variables. For reading of cards, this would require that the cards be punched in some way that would indicate where one number leaves off and another begins. A particularly simple way to do this is to require that each number be separated from adjacent numbers either by a comma or a blank column. With such a convention, numbers can be of any required length and need not be punched in fixed position on the card. That is, the first number on each of a group of cards might occupy five columns on the first card, seven columns on the second, two on the third, etc. Numbers can be punched with a decimal point if desired, and negative numbers can be indicated by punching a minus sign in front of the num-

ber. Figure 8.1 shows a card punched according to this system, with the four numbers being 12.754, −874, 0.000078, and −0.6664938. Note that it was punched on a card punch that prints the contents of each column at the top.

For output, the simple Print procedure would have to print numbers in a fixed format. Since the numbers to be printed could be of any size, it would be necessary to print them in *floating point* form, that is, as a decimal fraction times a power of ten. The conventional way to indicate the exponent is to precede it with the letter "E." If 20 printing positions are allowed for each number, the four numbers on the card of Figure 8.1 would print in this format as shown in Figure 8.2. The printers for most computers have 120 printing positions in a line, so that a maximum of six numbers per line could be printed with this scheme. If the Print procedure listed more than six quantities, additional lines would be printed.

Such a simplified system is entirely adequate for running practice problems while learning the basic ideas of algorithm writing. We feel, in fact, that it is much to be preferred that the beginner *not* become entangled in the details of a complete input and output system too early, lest the more important idea of the language of computing be obscured.

By now, however, these basic ideas should be fairly well in mind, and we turn to a brief consideration of something a little closer to computing world reality.

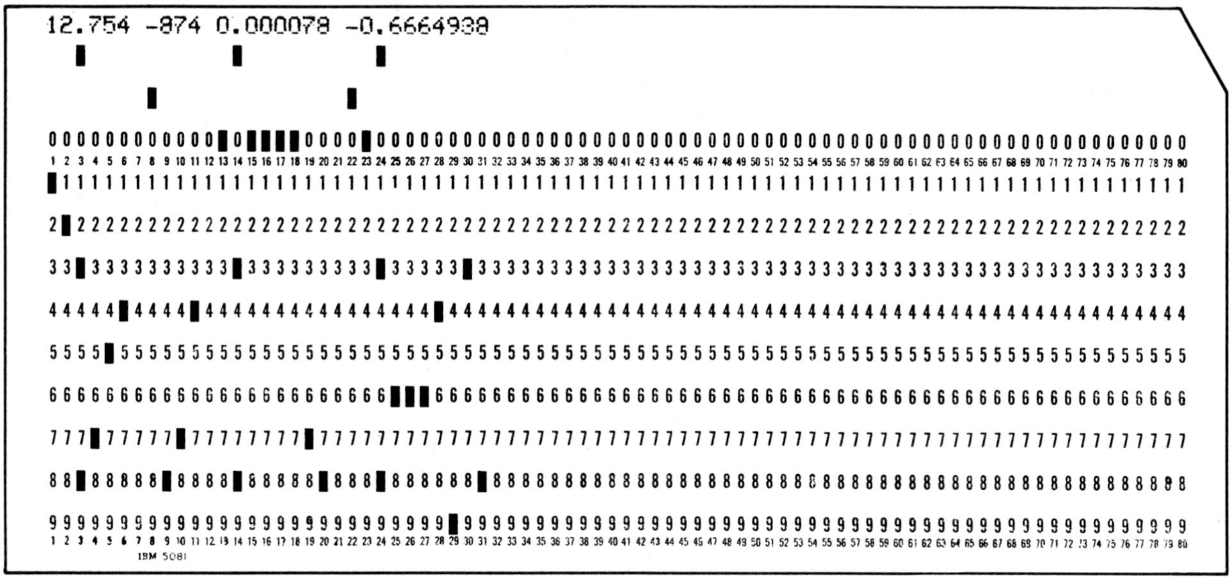

Figure 8.1. An example of a data card.

8.2 Input and Output in ALGOL

ALGOL was designed to be as independent of the characteristics of particular computers as possible. Since different machines differ widely in their input and output devices, it was decided not to include anything about the subject in the formal definition of the ALGOL language. Each writer of an ALGOL processor, therefore, must choose some system of input and output that is appropriate to his machine.

Since the various ALGOL processors will have different input and output characteristics, we cannot describe "the" ALGOL system and have it correct for every version of ALGOL. We have chosen to work with a hypothetical system, which, so far as is known, is not precisely the same as that for any actual processor. However, it is rather similar to the input and output capabilities of ALGOL for the Burroughs B5000 and not greatly different from the input and output characteristics of FORTRAN, a computer language somewhat similar to ALGOL.

8.3 The Format Declaration

The fundamental idea, which is common to all ALGOL and FORTRAN input and output systems, is that a *list* of variables is associated with a set of *field specifications* contained in a *format* declaration. This is the method of solution of the basic problem: how to tell the processor how much space is occupied by each number and how the number is written (with or without decimal points, with or without an exponent, etc.).

The format declaration is not a part of the basic ALGOL language; the processor must be designed to accept it accordingly. The simplest format declaration, as used here, takes the form

format identifier (field specifications) ;

The identifier is used to distinguish the various format declarations, since in most programs there will be many of them. The field specifications, which we shall consider in Section 8.4, are separated by commas if there is more than one—which is almost always.

```
0.12754000E 02      -0.87400000E 03      0.78000000E-04      -0.66649380E 00
```

Figure 8.2. A line printed from the data on the card in Figure 8.1. The numbers are in floating point format, with 20 spaces for each.

In the system assumed here every Read and Print procedure call must now contain as its first parameter a format declaration identifier.* The processor scans across the list of variables in the Read or Print statement, keeping in step with a similar scan of the field specifications in the format declaration to determine the format of each data field on a card or the format in which each number is to be printed.

Before considering the various field specifications in detail, let us look at a simple example. Suppose that five integer variables named $a, b, c, d,$ and e are to be printed, with four columns for a, five for b, six for c, and seven each for d and e. (The determination of the amount of space to be allowed for each number is the programmer's responsibility; enough space must be allowed to accommodate the largest value that could ever need to be printed.) It happens that the conventional way to designate an integer for printing is with the field specification "I," which is followed by a decimal number that dictates how many spaces are to be allowed for the number. We could therefore print the five integers with the two statements:

> **format** F1 (I4, I5, I6, I7, I7);
> Print (F1, a, b, c, d, e);

These work as follows. The format declaration is required to appear in the heading of some block. It does not by itself cause any action to take place in the object program. When the Print procedure call is encountered, the F1 specifies that the variables are to be printed according to the field specifications in the format declaration having the identifier F1. The list of variables is then scanned, from left to right, keeping in step with a similar scan of the field specifications in the referenced format declaration. The two statements would thus print a in four printing positions, b in five, c in six, and d and e in seven each. As we proceed, we shall see several extensions of this fundamental scheme of scanning.

*A system could be designed to make this requirement optional. If the first parameter was not a format identifier, which the processor could determine from the declarations elsewhere in the program, it would be assumed that the highly simplified input and output used heretofore in this book was desired. The same system could thus be used either for simple programs and student practice or for regular production computing.

8.4   Field Specifications

We shall discuss four types of field specifications, plus two other things that a format declaration may contain in our hypothetical but realistic input and output system. In each of the four types a complete field specification consists of the following:

1. A letter ($I, F, E,$ or B) to designate the type of information and something about how it is to be handled.

2. A number to designate how many card columns or printer spaces are involved.

The E and F field specifications require a second number to prescribe decimal-point handling.

To save repetition, we may note some facts that apply to each of the field specifications $I, F,$ and E.

On *input* a sign, if any, must be the first nonblank character of the field. The use of a plus sign is always optional; if no sign appears, the number is taken to be positive. Embedded blanks are taken to be zeros.

On *output* the number will appear at the right of the assigned field if more characters are specified for the field than there are characters in the number to be printed. If too few characters are specified, the sign and high-order digits will be lost. Plus signs are not printed.

In all four kinds it is permissible to specify that the same field specification applies to several successive fields by writing a *repetition number* in front of the field specification.

Field Specification I (Integer)

This is of the form Iw. I specifies conversion between an internal number of type integer and an external decimal integer. The total number of characters in the field, including sign and any blanks, is w. Decimal points are not permitted.

Field Specification F (External Fixed Point)

This is of the form F$w.d$. The F indicates conversion between an internal number of type real and an external number written without an exponent. The total number of characters in the field, including sign, decimal point, and any blanks, is w. The number of places after the (assumed) decimal point is d.

On *input* the use of an actual decimal point is optional: if one is supplied, it overrides d. Shown below are some sample data fields and the numbers to which they would be converted if read under control of F10.6.

Data Field	Converted Internal Number
$+12345678$	$+12.345678$
1234.5678	$+1234.5678$
-1.2345678	-1.2345678
$.012345678$	$+.012345678$
-1.2	-1.2
$+1234567$	$+1.234567$
123	$+.000123$

On *output* there will be d places to the right of the decimal point. For example, consider the real numbers 1.2345678, 12.345678, and -123.45678. With the field specification F11.5, they would print as

```
1.23457   12.34568  -123.45678
```

Note that each number has been rounded to five decimal places and that each occupies a total of 11 spaces. With the field specification F8.2 they would appear as

```
   1.23    12.35   -123.46
```

If the field specification F8.5 were used, there would be trouble because there would not be enough space to contain the numbers. The result would be

```
   1.2345712.3456823.45678
```

This illustrates that when using the F field specification it is essential to know the maximum sizes of all numbers, a problem that is avoided when the E field specification is used.

Field Specification E (Floating Point)

This is of the form E$w.d$. E specifies conversion between an internal real number and an external number written with an exponent. The total number of characters in the field in the external medium is w, including sign, decimal point, exponent, and any blanks. The number of places after the decimal point (not counting the exponent) is d.

On *input* the use of an actual decimal point is optional; if one is supplied, it overrides d. The exponent part of the field is of the general form $E \pm ee$, which is similar to one transliterated form of the exponent in a real number in a statement.

Actual processors would in most cases permit some shortcuts in writing exponents to simplify card punching. A positive exponent could appear with the $+$ omitted or replaced with a blank, that is, in the form E ee or Eee. If the first digit of the exponent is zero, it may be omitted. If the exponent is written with a sign, the E may be omitted. Thus the following are permissible (and equivalent) ways of writing the exponent *plus 2:* $E + 02$, $E\ 02$, $E02$, $E + 2$, $E2$, $+02$, $+2$.

For example, observe that the following four data fields convert to the same internal number if read in under the control of E14.7 (remember that an actual decimal point overrides d in the field specification):

$$+12345678E03 \qquad 1234.5678E0$$
$$12345678.E - 4 \qquad +0.12345678 + 4$$

On *output* the number will normally appear in the form $\pm 0.nn \cdots E \pm ee$ (except that plus signs are replaced with blanks), where the number of places after the decimal point is specified by d.

Field Specification B (Blank)

This is of the form Bw. It causes the insertion of w blank spaces in a line of printing, between the printing positions for the preceding and following numbers. The same thing can always be accomplished by providing the same number of additional spaces in the field specification of the following field, but this is sometimes inconvenient.

Strings

It is frequently desirable in printing results to provide various kinds of identification, such as column headings, problem or data identification, explanatory comments, etc. Such information can be printed by inserting a *string* in the format statement. A string is simply any set of the characters available on the computer, enclosed in quotation marks.[*] The characters in the string are printed in the position in the line indicated by the position of the string in the format statement. The string does not correspond to any variable in the list of the Print that references the format statement. Instead, the string itself is printed. No indication of the presence of the string is required in the Print. Whenever the string is encountered in the scanning of the format statement, the text of the string is written out, and scanning continues with-

[*] Or some transliteration of the quotation marks, typically asterisks.

out any variable from the list having been transmitted. It is possible to print a line consisting entirely of text by putting nothing but a string in the format declaration and listing no variables in the Print procedure call.

Printer Carriage Control

We have assumed throughout that lines of printing are single spaced, which is what happens if nothing to the contrary is indicated. Frequently, however, it is necessary to do something different; most often, we wish either to double space or to skip to the top of the next page. In the system assumed here, these actions are called for by writing either *double* or *page,* respectively, as the first thing in the format declaration. (Actual input/output systems usually provide considerably more than this in the way of carriage control, but the details vary so much that it would be difficult even to summarize them. Furthermore, the beginning programmer would seldom need these capabilities.)

8.5   Additional List Features

So far we have discussed Read and Print calls in which each variable is named explicitly. This would obviously not be convenient when an array is to be read or printed. For this purpose we are permitted to write variables with subscripts; a scheme similar to the for-step-until construction then provides for stepping through the elements of the array.

List indexing can be specified in a number of ways in the Read or Print call. Probably the most direct is to imitate the action of the for-step-until rather directly, as in the following example:

Print (**for** i : = 1 **step** 1 **until** 5 **do** x [i]);

In a rather obvious interpretation, this calls for the printing of the first five elements of the array named X. It is permissible to use all of the normal facilities of the for-statement with a step-until for-list, such as nesting, a step value other than 1, and indexing parameters that are themselves variables.

This does raise a new and important question, however: what happens if more values are listed than can be contained in one card or one line of printing? Let us begin to answer this question by noting that any input or output operation *always* implies starting with the leftmost position of a

new card or line. If there are six numbers punched on a card, it is impossible to read them with two Reads, the second taking up where the first left off. Next, we should note that whenever the closing parenthesis of the format declaration is encountered, the program moves on to a new card or page, even if space remains in the one at hand. Thus, if we have five numbers to be printed, all with the same field specification of E20.8, and we wrote the format declaration

format F (E20.8);

the five numbers would be printed on *five lines.* To get them all on one line, the format declaration must contain five field specifications; if they are all the same, it is convenient to use a repetition number:

format F (5E20.8);

The final part of the answer to the question above is that whenever list variables remain when the end of a card or line is reached, whether or not the closing parenthesis of the format declaration has been reached, the program moves on to a new card or new line.

For an example of all this, suppose we wanted to print the 20 elements of an array named R on four lines, five to each line. The Print call has no concern with the arrangement on the page:

Print (**for** i : = 1 **step** 1 **until** 20 **do** R [i]);

The format declaration should have a repetition number of 5: after repeating the field specification five times, the closing parenthesis of the format will be reached, causing printing to start over with a new line and causing scanning of the format declaration to begin again at the beginning.

We may note that in the case of output there is no restriction to single variables. In most systems any arithmetic expression may be written; it is the value of the expression that is printed. In particular, it is permissible to write numbers in the list of a Print, causing the numbers themselves to be printed. Note, however, that this is not the same as writing a string in a format statement. In the case of the string the characters in the string are printed exactly as they are written; in the case of numbers in a list the numbers are printed as dictated by the corresponding field specification. It could happen, for instance, that writing the digit 1 in a list would result in printing 0.10000000E 01.

One final note on lists. It is permissible to use

a variable in the list as a subscript in the same list. This means, typically, that an element of an array can be punched on a card with its element number; a single Read call will cause it to be stored in the proper place in its array. A typical call would be:

$$\text{Read } (i, j, a\,[i, j])\,;$$

The data card would have to be punched with the row number first, then the column number, then the element. It should be clear that variables used in this way for input must appear earlier in the list as variables than as subscripts (otherwise old or nonexistent values would be involved). For output, there is no such restriction.

8.6 Additional Format Features

Just as it is possible to repeat a field specification by writing a repetition number in front of it, it is also possible to repeat a group of field specifications. The group is enclosed in parentheses, and the desired number of repetitions is written before it. For instance, suppose that eight fields on a card are alternately described by I2 and F10.0. We can write 4(I2, F10.0) to get the desired action. This is *not* the same as 4I2, 4F10.0, which would describe a card with four I2 fields followed by four F10.0 fields rather than the desired alternation.

When the list of an input or output operation is used to transmit more than one *record* (card or line), with the different records having different formats, a slash (/) is used to separate the format specifications of the different records. For example, suppose that two cards are to be read with a single Read call; the first card has only a four-digit integer and the second has six real numbers. We could write

format H12 (I4/6E14.0);

It is possible to specify a special format for the first one or more records and a different format from the first group for all subsequent records. This is done by enclosing the last record specifications in parentheses. For instance, if the first card of a deck has an integer and a real number and all following contain two integers and a real number, we could write

format form (I4, E14.0/(2I4, E14.0));

A slash always indicates the end of one record and the beginning of a new one, just as the closing parenthesis does. The skipping of entire records (on the printer, usually) is called for by writing successive slashes. Note that the skipping of n records is called for by writing $n + 1$ successive slashes.

A *scale factor* may be used with the E field specification on output by writing the field specification in the form sPnEw.d, where s is the scale factor, P stands for "place" or "point," and n is the repetition number. The effect of the scale factor is to move the decimal point s places to the right and decrease the exponent by s.

For an example, suppose there are three numbers that under control of 3E17.8 would print as shown in the first line of Figure 8.3. The same numbers printed under control of 3E12.3 would print as shown in the second line. Printed under control of 1P3E11.4, the numbers would appear as shown in the third line. Notice that by allowing only the minimum number of spaces we have crowded the printing, making it difficult to read.

For routine printing of numbers of the real type, the most common field specification is probably 1PE20.7. This prints the decimal point in the familiar position between the first and second digits, prints all significant figures available in most ALGOL systems, and provides plenty of space for easy reading.

```
0.12345678E 03   -0.55555555E 00   0.87654321E-05


0.123E 03   -0.556E 00   0.877E-05


1.2346E 02-5.5556E-01 8.7654E-06
```

Figure 8.3. Three ways of printing the same numbers, showing the effect of different field specifications.

ACCELERATION CALCULATION

X=	4.9143062E-02	Y=	-6.1243299E 05
X=	6.1462201E-02	Y=	-9.4016230E 05
X=	8.9001657E-02	Y=	-2.6033842E 06
X=	1.1297321E-01	Y=	-5.5610328E 07
X=	5.0163284E-01	Y=	-9.8632141E 07
X=	8.6489962E-01	Y=	-4.1126813E 08

Figure 8.4. Sample output produced by the program segment of Figure 8.5.

8.7 Examples

A few examples may help to clarify some of the ideas regarding the use of format declarations to accomplish desired results.

Suppose that we wish to read a deck of cards containing elements of a one-dimensional array named *data*. The first card contains only the value of a number n, punched in columns 1–2, which specifies how many cards there are in the rest of the deck. Each remaining card contains an element number in 1–2 and the value of the element in 3–15 in a form for reading with E13.0. The deck can be read and each element stored in the proper location with the following format declaration and Read procedure call:

> **format** F56 (I2/(I2, E13.0));
> Read (F56, n, **for** i := 1 **step** 1 **until** n **do**
>   **begin** k, data [k] **end**);

In the format declaration the slash says that the first card contains only one integer. The parentheses around I2, E13.0 will cause repeated scanning of those two field specifications. In the Read the F56 is the format identifier; the n goes with the first I2; indexing is used to read just n cards. The use of i as the indexing parameter and k as the variable subscript is no mistake: we want to repeat the reading of cards containing an integer and a real number exactly n times, but there is no assumption that the integers on those cards run in order from 1 to n. In other words, the elements may not be in the deck in proper order; with this arrangement, it doesn't matter.

For a second example suppose that an output page is to be printed with a page heading and column identifications as shown in Figure 8.4. Note that there are two blank lines between the heading and the body. The "X=" and "Y=" are obtained

with strings in the format, as is the heading. The X and Y values are the elements of two one-dimensional arrays of six elements each. The statements to do all this are shown in Figure 8.5.

We have here an example of a Print call without a list of variables. The format for printing the heading contains only string text and the three slashes to skip two lines, but no field specifications. The second Print uses list indexing to specify the six elements of each array. The second format illustrates several features. The X values will be printed under control of 1PE16.7. Recall that "1P" will move the decimal point one place to the right and adjust the exponent accordingly. In "##Y=" the symbol # is used as the conventional indication of a blank space. These blanks are necessary to avoid having the Y= print immediately adjacent to the previous X value, which would make the report difficult to read.

Let us now investigate briefly the kind of Print and format arrangements used to produce the output samples reproduced elsewhere in the book.*

First consider the results of the quadratic equation program shown in Figure 1.6. The output statements should arrange to skip to a new page before printing the column headings and double space everything. The data and results are to be printed with three decimal places and no exponent, every number being allowed ten printing positions. The number of roots is a one-digit integer, but six positions are allowed for it to improve readability. All this is done simply enough with the segment shown in Figure 8.6.

Next consider the output of the quadrilateral analysis program results shown in Figure 3.9. The

---

* More precisely, *would* have been used if the printing had been done according to the scheme presented here. In fact, it was done in slightly different form with a processor for an existing computer.

format G ('ACCELERATION CALCULATION' ///);
format H ('X =' 1PE16.7, '##Y =' 1PE16.7);

Print (G);
Print (H, **for** i : = 1 **step** 1 **until** 6 **do**
      begin X [i], Y [i] **end**);

Figure 8.5. Format declarations and Print procedure call to print the output of Figure 8.4. The formats would have to be in the head of the block containing the calls. The symbol # is used to denote positions that should be left blank in punching the cards of the program.

two tolerances are to be printed on a separate line at the top of a new page. Each line of output consists of an integer case number, eight real numbers with two decimal places, eight blank spaces, and a word to identify the type of geometrical figure. The format declarations for this job are shown in Figure 8.7. Note the convenience of the B field specification: without it, we would have had to insert blanks into each string. (It should be realized that in an attempt to keep the program of Figure 3.8 simple a shortcut was taken: the string was inserted in the list instead of in a format declaration. Although this method is contrary to the system described in this chapter, it could presumably be implemented.)

8.8 Other Input and Output Devices

In this book we have spoken exclusively of reading cards and printing lines. There are, however, a number of other input and output devices, some of which are more or less frequently used in connection with ALGOL programs.

Many computers have a device for punching cards; a few can *only* punch cards instead of being able to print lines on a page. Card punching is a rather slow process to be avoided if there is any satisfactory substitute.

Some computers have a typewriter instead of, or in addition to, a printer. Only the smaller computers have a typewriter as the only printing device, since typing is slow compared with printing an entire line at a time, the ratio being in the neighborhood of a hundred to one for a full line of (generally) 120 characters. A number of the larger machines have both a line printer and a typewriter. The line printer is used for volume results and the typewriter mostly for comments and instructions to the operator.

Some machines, typically the smaller ones, are able to read punched paper tape and to punch it. An input tape must be prepared on a special typewriter designed for the purpose, or tape previously punched on the computer can be read. Output tapes can be printed on the same special typewriter. Paper tape can be read at approximately the same speed as cards or a little slower; it can be punched faster than typing but much slower than line printing. It is far slower than magnetic tape.

A few machines can be equipped with a cathode ray tube (TV) display device. This can be used for visual displays of graphs and text; if it is provided with a camera, it can produce permanent records.

The most important input and output device besides a card reader and a printer is magnetic tape. This is available without exception for all

format heading (PAGE, '#######A########B########C
     #####X1REAL####X1IMAG####X2REAL####X2IMAG###ROOTS');
format body (DOUBLE, 7F10.3, I6);

Print (heading);
Print (body, a, b, c, x1real, x1imag, x2real, x2imag, Roots);

Figure 8.6. Format declarations and Print calls to produce the output of Figure 1.6.

format L1 (PAGE, 'ANGTOLER' F10.4, 5B, 'SIDETOLER' F10.4//);
format L2 ('CASE' 2B, 'AB' 6B, 'BC' 6B, 'CD' 6B, 'AD' 6B, 'ABC' 5B,
　　　　'BCD' 5B, 'ADC' 5B, 'BAD' 11B, 'FIGURE'//);
format square (I3, 8F8.2, B8, 'SQUARE');
format rectangle (I3, 8F8.2, B8, 'RECTANGLE');
format rhombus (I3, 8F8.2, B8, 'RHOMBUS');
format parallelogram (I3, 8F8.2, B8, 'PARALLELOGRAM');
format none (I3, 8F8.2, B8, 'NONE');

Figure 8.7. Format declarations to produce the output of Figure 3.9.

large computers and for most small ones as well, although the smaller machines are not always equipped with it even though it is available. Magnetic tape is utilized in two rather different ways; the more common application is in speeding input and output.

Reading cards at a few hundred a minute is slow compared with the internal arithmetic speed of a large computer, and printing is little better. Therefore, except when the amount of input and output is small, the usual procedure is to use magnetic tape to reduce the wasted computer time. This is done, in the case of input, by first taping the information on the cards with a separate card-to-tape converter that is not connected to the computer. While this is being done, the computer can be used for other work. When the problem is ready to be run, the magnetic tape is mounted on a tape unit that is connected to the computer, and the problem data is read in at about a hundred times the speed of card reading.

Similarly, problem results are written on magnetic tape rather than directly printed. When the problem is completed, the output tape is moved from the computer to a separate tape unit connected to a printer. The results are then printed while the computer is engaged in other work.

This perhaps sounds like more trouble than it is. In practice, the whole operation runs very smoothly, and the programmer ordinarily has nothing to do with the mechanics of the tape handling. (In many installations *all* computer operating is done by specialists in such work; some programmers have never so much as touched a computer.) The net result is a considerable increase in computer efficiency.

The other, less common, use of magnetic tape provides intermediate storage for results during the solution of a problem. For instance, some problems involve large arrays, which may be too big to fit in computer storage at one time. In such a case the intermediate results can be written on magnetic tape as they are computed and read back in when they are needed.

A few computers have magnetic drums that are used for intermediate storage in the same way that magnetic tapes are. (This is distinct from the machine in which a magnetic drum is the primary storage device.) Drums are in about the same speed range as magnetic tapes but of much smaller capacity.

No computer would be likely to have all these devices. A typical small machine has a typewriter for typing in minor amounts of data and for typing out results, plus a paper tape reader and punch. A typical medium-to-large machine has a card reader, a line printer, a few to a dozen magnetic tapes that may be used either for input and output or for intermediate storage, and perhaps a typewriter.

Writing programs to work with these various input and output devices requires some additional language features to specify the device to be employed and, in some cases, to provide the additional information they need. These additional language elements can be built up in two ways. In one class of ALGOL system there are just two input and output procedures: Read and Write. The choice of a particular device is indicated as one of the parameters on the call or by a separate description of the file (collection of information) that is to be read or written. The designation of an input or output device can be made conditional upon a control card that is read at the start of a problem run; this makes it possible to change the choice of input or output medium rather simply, without reprogramming. (For instance, it might be desirable to switch from the normal tape output to printer output when only a few lines of printing are expected for a certain set of data.)

The other way to specify the device to be used is to provide additional procedure calls for the various devices, such as punch, type, read paper tape, write paper tape, read drum, write drum, read tape, write tape, read input tape, write output tape, backspace, rewind, etc. This method seems to be in somewhat wider use.

EXERCISES

*1. Four numbers are punched on a card; they are new values of real variables named BOS, EWR, PHL, and DCA. Each number is punched in eight columns, with a decimal point. Write Read and format statements to read the card.

2. Same as Exercise 1, except that there is no decimal point. The numbers are to be treated as if they had two decimal places, that is, two places to the right of an assumed decimal point.

3. Same as Exercise 1, except that each number occupies 14 columns and is punched with an exponent (and a decimal point).

*4. A Card is punched in the following format.

Columns	Sample Format	Associated Variable Name
1–3	± xx	LGA
4–6	xxx	IDL
7–20	± x.xxxxxxxE ± ee	BAL
21–34	± x.xxxxxxxE ± ee	ATL

The small letters stand for any digits. Write statements to read such a card.

*5. *Data* is a one-dimensional array of at most ten elements. A card is punched with a value of N in columns 1–2 and with one to ten elements of *data* in succeeding columns. The number of elements is given by the value of N. Each number is punched with a decimal point but no exponent, in seven columns. Write statements to read such a card.

6. Same as Exercise 5, except that the numbers are the *odd*-numbered elements of *data*; there are therefore at most five of them. N is the *element number* of the last one, not the total number of elements.

*7. M is a two-dimensional array of integer numbers, with three rows and four columns. A card is punched with the 12 elements of M, each integer taking three columns. Write statements to read such a card, after deciding the most advantageous order for the elements to appear on the card.

8. L is a three-dimensional array named in the declaration

real array L [1:2, 1:2, 1:3];

A card is punched with the 12 elements of L, each integer taking three columns. Write statements to read such a card, after specifying the order in which they should be punched on the card.

*9. The values of the variables A, B, X, and Z are to be printed on one line. A and B are to be printed without exponents, X and Z with. Twelve spaces should be allowed for A and B, and they should have four decimal places. Twenty spaces should be allowed for X and Z, and they should be printed in the normal form with eight decimal places. Write appropriate statements.

10. Same as Exercise 9, except that a positive integer named K is to be printed in six spaces between A and B, and the decimal point is to be moved one place to the right in X and Z.

*11. A two-dimensional array named ABC consists of ten rows and four columns. Write a program segment to print the following on a page. At the top of the page is the heading "MATRIX ABC." The elements are then printed in the normal row-and-column arrangement for a two-dimensional array, using E20.8 field specifications. (*Hint.* Be sure that exactly four numbers are printed on each line.)

12. A one-dimensional array named CVG contains a maximum of 40 elements. The input deck has one card per element; each card has the element number in columns 1–2 and the element itself in columns 3–12, punched with a decimal point but without an exponent. The cards may not be assumed to be in correct order. It is not known how many cards there are; the last card of the deck is blank, which will look like an element number of zero. Write a program segment to read the deck and store each element in the correct location in the array.

13. A two-dimensional array PHX is named in the declaration

real array PHX [1:10, 1:13];

The actual number of rows and columns is given by the values of the variables M and N, respectively. Write a program segment to print as many elements as there actually are, in row order. Each element is to be printed on a separate line along with its row and column numbers. Use I2 for the integers and 1PE20.7 for the real numbers.

ANSWERS TO SELECTED EXERCISES

There are several acceptable answers to many of these exercises. Sometimes the one shown here is ~~~~~~~~~~~~ ~~~~~~~~~~ly are we able

$A = B + C$ or $A = C + B$. In short, the answers given here are correct but usually not unique.

The general idea is to provide you with a way of checking your over-all approach. If your solution is different from that given here but produces the same results with about the same amount of effort, your answer will be accepted.

```
*  24
*                      TXL        5.25
*                     SBTL        5.25
*     076              TAX        0.37
*                  03 TOT        $5.62
          001 10⧧12⧧73 CASH
*
*                 CHCK  TND      $5.62
*                       CHNG     $0.00
      MCGRAW HILL          THANK YOU
```

3.

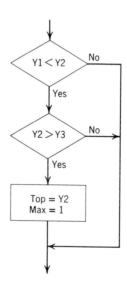

4.

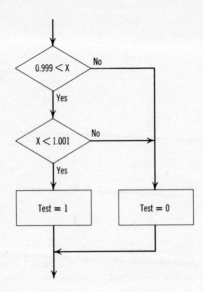

A better way is to use absolute value:

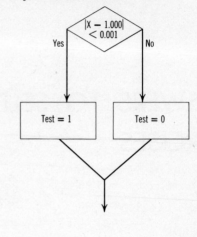

5. $x_1 = L \cos A$
$y_1 = L \sin A$

7.

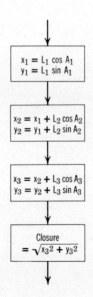

10.

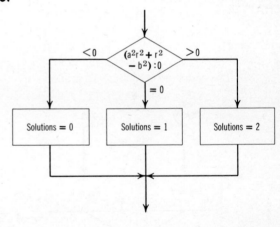

11.

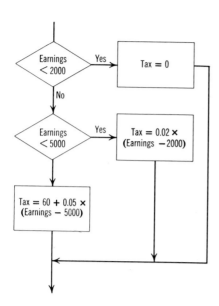

12.

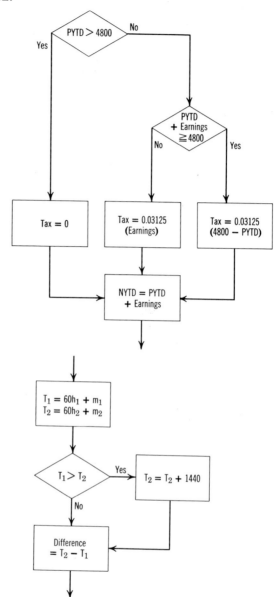

15. Best to get both times in minutes since midnight, as shown in first box. Then comes the catch in this problem: the two times may not have been in the same day. Since we are guaranteed that they are less than 24 hours apart and that the first one actually is earlier than the second, we can detect this condition by asking if $T_1 > T_2$. If this happens, we can correct for it by adding 1440 minutes (= 24 hours) to the second time and proceeding.

CHAPTER 2

1. Yes.

2. 42Y, 1X2, 2a, and 158 are incorrect because they start with a digit. x + 3, A/M (square), and T1.4 are wrong because they contain a character other than a letter or a digit. g^{-1} and B_7 are wrong because superscripts and subscripts are not allowed. arctan is a function name; begin and while would be reserved words in some systems.

3. c. $x \uparrow 1.667$
 f. $A + B/(C + D)$
 h. $(A + B)/(C + D) + X1 \uparrow 2$
 i. $(A + B)/(C + D/(F + G))$
 j. $1 + x + x \uparrow 2/2 + x \uparrow 3/6$
 l. $x/(1 + x \uparrow 2/(3 + (2 \times x) \uparrow 2/(5 + (3 \times x) \uparrow 2/(7 + (4 \times x) \uparrow 2))))$
 m. $a \times b + c \uparrow d - 2 \uparrow x \uparrow 2$

4. b. $(x + 2)/(y + 4)$
 d. $((X + A + 3.1416)/(2 \times Z)) \uparrow 2$
 f. $a/b + c \times d/(e \times f \times g)$
 i. $(1600042 \times G + 1_{10}5)/(4568995 \times G + 1_{10}5)$

5. d. $A + B \uparrow (i + 2) \times B/C$
 f. $a \times b/(c \times d/(e \times f))$
 i. $(A + B + C \times D \uparrow 2)/(((A + 7.9) \uparrow (i - 1) + B/(C + D)) \times (A + 6))$

CHAPTER 3

1. a. **if** a $>$ b **then** x $:=$ 16.9 **else** y $:=$ 23.1;

c. **go to if** rho $+$ theta $<$ $_{10}$ $-$ 6 **then** alldone **else** oncemore;

e. signs $:=$ **if** g $<$ 0 $\wedge$ h $<$ 0 **then** -1 **else if** g $>$ 0 $\wedge$ h $>$ 0 **then** $+1$ **else** 0;

f. **go to if** 0.999 $<$ x $\wedge$ x $<$ 1.001 **then** wrapup **else** start new iteration;

Better: **go to if** abs (x $-$ 1.000) $<$ 0.001 **then** wrapup **else** start new iteration;

h. **go to if** i $=$ 1 $\wedge$ R $<$ S **then** 261 **else if** i $=$ 1 **then** 257 **else** 297; Note that with this sequence of testing it is not necessary to include the conditions R $\geqq$ S and i $\neq$ 1.

j. **if** i $=$ 1 **then go to** first **else if** 1 $<$ i $\wedge$ i $<$ n **then go to** between **else if** i $=$ n **then go to** last; Note that the problem statement does not say what to do if i is less than 1 or greater than n; we assume in this solution that *nothing* is to be done. On this assumption, it is not possible to use a go-to-if construction, since such a form is required to have the **else** at the end.

k. Big $:=$ **if** X $<$ Y **then** Y **else** X;

m. **if** abs (Xreal) $<$ 1 $\wedge$ abs (Ximag) $<$ 1 **then go to** square;

2. a. P $:=$ **if** m $>$ 0 **then** 1.5708 $\times$ exp $(-m)$
        else if m $=$ 0 **then** 0
        else 1.5708 $\times$ exp (m);

Also possible:
    P $:=$ **if** m $=$ 0 **then** 0 **else**
        1.5708 $\times$ exp $(-m \times$ sign (m));

c. switchg $:=$ **if** k $<$ 0 **then** 1
        else if k $=$ 0 **then** 2 **else** 3;

Better: switchg $:=$ 2 $+$ sign (k);

3.   **begin real** x, y;
        x $:=$ 1.0;
  again: y $:=$ 16.7 $\times$ x $+$ 9.2 $\times$ x $\uparrow$ 2 $-$ 1.02
           $\times$ x $\uparrow$ 3;
        Print (x, y);
        x $:=$ x $+$ 0.1;
        if x $<$ 10.0 **then go to** again;
        Stop
        end

5. begin real A1, A2, A3, A4, L1, L2, L3, L4,
    x, y, OK;
  x $:=$ L1 $\times$ cos (A1) $+$ L2 $\times$ cos (A2)
    $+$ L3 $\times$ cos (A3) $+$ L4 $\times$ cos (A4);
  y $:=$ L1 $\times$ sin (A1) $+$ L2 $\times$ sin (A2)
    $+$ L3 $\times$ sin (A3)
    $+$ L4 $\times$ sin (A4);
  OK $:=$ **if** sqrt (x $\uparrow$ 2 $+$ y $\uparrow$ 2) $<$ 0.01 $\times$
    (L1 $+$ L2 $+$ L3 $+$ L4)
    $\wedge$ L1 $\neq$ 0 $\wedge$ L2 $\neq$ 0 $\wedge$ L3 $\neq$ 0 $\wedge$ L4 $\neq$ 0
    then 1 **else** 0
end
The computation could be arranged in many other ways.

7. begin real a, b, r, Solutions;
  Solutions $:=$ 1 $+$ sign (a $\uparrow$ 2 $\times$ r $\uparrow$ 2 $+$ r $\uparrow$ 2
    $-$ b $\uparrow$ 2)
end

If this were to be used in a practical program, the test would probably have to be set up so that a discriminant very close to zero would be accepted as indicating tangency.

10.   **begin real** x, a, b, n, h, Trapezoidal,
        sum;
    h $:=$ (b $-$ a)/n;
    sum $:=$ 0;
    x $:=$ a $+$ h;
  here: sum $:=$ sum $+$ sqrt (x)
        $\times$ sin (x)/(x $+$ exp (x));
    x $:=$ x $+$ h;
    if x $<$ b **then go to** here;
    Trapezoidal $:=$ h/2 $\times$ (sqrt (a)
        $\times$ sin (a)/(a $+$ exp (a))
        $+$ 2 $\times$ sum $+$ sqrt (b) $\times$ sin (b)/
        (b $+$ exp (b)))
    end

CHAPTER 4

1. a. **for** x $:=$ 1.1 **step** 0.1 **until** 1.9 **do**
    begin
        y $:=$ x $-$ sin (x)/cos (x);
        Print (x, y)
    end

c. root $:=$ sqrt (a $\uparrow$ 2 $+$ b $\uparrow$ 2);
  for x $:=$ 0.1, 0.6 **step** 0.1 **until** 1.0 **do**
    begin
        y $:=$ 1/(a $\times$ root) $\times$ arctan (a $\times$
           sin (x)/cos (x)/root);
        Print (x, y)
    end

e. sum $:=$ 0;
  term $:=$ 1;
  for n $:=$ 1 **step** 1 **until** 20 **do**
    begin

```
              sum : = sum + term;
              term : = term × x/n
           end
    f. sum : = n : = 0;
       term : = 1;
       for n : = n + 1 while term > $_{10}-6$ × sum
           do begin
              sum : = sum + term;
              term : = term × x/n
           end
    j. Pi : = 2;
       for i : = 2 step 2 until 150 do
           Pi : = Pi × i↑2/((i − 1) × (i + 1));
    l. x : = 0;
       for x : = x + 0.1 while
              exp (−b × x) ≧ 0.001 do
           begin
           y : = a × exp (−b × x);
```

```
           Print (x, y)
        end
    n. for a : = 1.0 step 0.1 until 1.9 do
       for b : = 1 step 1 until 20 do
           begin
           y : = sqrt ((3.14159 × a) ↑ 2 + 1/b)
                    + exp (−a/2)/(b + 6);
           Print (a, b, y)
        end
 3. begin integer N, T;
    T : = 1;
    for T : = T + 2 while T ↑ 2 ≦ N do
        if N − (N ÷ T) × T = 0
           then go to NotPrime;
        Print (N);
    NotPrime: (((Whatever follows)))
    end
```

CHAPTER 5

```
1. a. begin real distance; real array x [1:3];
       distance : = sqrt (x [1] ↑ 2 + x [2] ↑ 2 + x [3] ↑ 2)
    end
   c. begin real D; integer i; real array a, b [1:30];
      D : = 0;
      for i : = 1 step 1 until 30 do
      D : = D + (a [i] − b [i]) ↑ 2
      end
   e. begin real sum; integer i; real array data [1:78];
      sum : = 0;
      for i : = 2 step 3 until 78 do
      sum : = sum + data [i]
      end
   h. begin real trapezoidal, sum; integer i; real array Y [1:32];
      sum : = 0;
      for i : = 2 step 1 until 31 do
           sum : = sum + Y [i];
      trapezoidal : = Y [1] + 2 × sum + Y [32]
      end
   j. begin Boolean greater; real array a, b [1:23]; integer i;
      greater : = true;
      for i : = 1 step 1 until 23 do
           if a [i] ≦ b [i] then begin greater : = false; go to out end;
      out: (((whatever follows)))
      end
   k. begin integer i, Nbig; real Big; real array vector [1:20];
      Big : = vector [1];
      Nbig : = 1;
      for i : = 2 step 1 until 20 do
           if vector [i] > Big then begin Big : = vector [i]; Nbig : = i end
      end
```

```
m.  begin real Big; integer i, j, Nbig; array vector [1:20];
    for i : = 1 step 1 until 19 do
            begin
            Big : = vector [i];
            Nbig : = i;
            for j : = i + 1 step 1 until 20 do
                    if vector [j] > Big then
                            begin
                            Big : = vector [j];
                            Nbig : = j
                            end;
            if Nbig ≠ i then
                    begin
                    vector [Nbig] : = vector [i];
                    vector [i] : = Big
                    end
            end
    end
o.  begin real heavy; integer i, j, row, column;
            real array influence [1:7, 1:17];
    heavy : = influence [1, 1];
    row : = column : = 1;
    for i : = 1 step 1 until 7 do
    for j : = 1 step 1 until 17 do
            if influence [i, j] > heavy then
                    begin
                    heavy : = influence [i, j];
                    row : = i;
                    column : = j
                    end
    end
q.  begin real array R, S, T [1:40]; integer i, M;
    for i : = 1 step 1 until M do
            T [i] : = R [i] + S [i]
    end
r.  begin real array F [1:50]; integer i, M;
    for i : = 2 step 1 until M − 1 do
            F [i] : = (F [i − 1] + F [i] + F [i + 1])/3
    end
t.  begin real xs, ys; integer i; real array X, Y [1:50];
    for i : = 1 step 1 until 50 do
            if xs = X [i] then begin ys : = Y [i]; go to out end;
    out: (((whatever follows)))
    end
x.  begin real array a, b, c [1:15, 1:15]; integer i, j, k;
    for i : = 1 step 1 until 15 do
    for j : = 1 step 1 until 15 do
    begin
    c [i, j] : = 0;
    for k : = 1 step 1 until 15 do
    c [i, j] : = c [i, j] + a [i, k] × b [k, j]
    end
    end
```

CHAPTER 6

1.

b. **switch** b : = first, second, third, fourth;

   go to b [n ÷ 10 + 1];
   first: y : = r × exp (x + 1.117); **go to** continue;
   second: y : = s × exp (x + 1.57); **go to** continue;
   third: y : = t × exp (x + 2.89); **go to** continue;
   fourth: y : = u × exp (x + 3.04); **go to** continue;
   continue: (((whatever follows)))

d. **switch** d : = 40, 41, 42, 43, 44;

   go to d [entier(k)];
   40: y : = g; **go to** more;
   41: y : = g × x; **go to** more;
   42: y : = g × x ↑ 2 + h; **go to** more;
   43: y : = g × x ↑ 3 + h × x + i; **go to** more;
   44: y : = g × x ↑ 4 + h × x ↑ 2 + i × x;
   more: (((whatever follows)))

2. b.

	A	B	C	D
u	L	G	G	G
v	U	L	U	U
w	U	U	L	U
x	U	U	U	L

c.

	A	B	C	D	E	F
g	L	G	G	G	G	G
h	U	L	G	G	G	U
i	U	U	L	U	U	U
j	U	U	U	L	G	U
k	U	U	U	U	L	U
l	U	U	U	U	U	L

3. b. A: **begin real** a, b, c, x, asq, xsq, h, i, j, k;
               Read (a, b, c, x);
               asq : = a ↑ 2; xsq : = x ↑ 2;

   B: **begin real** root1;
               root1 : = sqrt (asq − xsq);

   C: **begin real** log;
                   log : = ln (a);
                   h : = root1 × log + abs (log)/(root1 + 1)
                   end C;

   D: **begin real** bsq;
                   bsq : = b ↑ 2;
                   i : = bsq × root1 + 3/(bsq ↑ 2 × root1)
                         −arctan (x/a)/bsq
                   end D
               end B;

   E: **begin real** root2;
               root2 : = sqrt (xsq + asq);

   F: **begin real** csq;
                   csq : = c ↑ 2;
                   j : = root2 ↑ 5/5 − 2 × csq × root2 ↑ 3/3
                         + csq ↑ 2 × root2
                   end F;

```
G:                          begin real xcube;
                            xcube := x ↑ 3;
                            k := −xcube ↑ 2/root2 − xcube/(3 × root2 ↑ 3)
                                   +ln (x + root2)
                            end G
                      end E;
              Print (a, b, c, x, h, i, j, k)
              end A;
  d. begin real a, b, x, p, q, r, s, asq, bsq;
     Read (a, b, x);
     asq := a ↑ 2;
     bsq := b ↑ 2;
          begin real T1;
          T1 := sqrt (asq + x ↑ 2);
          p := a × T1 + b/T1;
          q := asq × T1 ↑ 3 − bsq × T1 + a × b/T1
          end;
          begin real T1;
          T1 := a − x;
          r := a × ln (T1) + b × T1 ↑ 3;
          s := a ↑ 3 × bsq × T1 ↑ (1/3)
          end;
     Print (a, b, x, p, q, r, s)
     end
```

CHAPTER 7

1. real procedure denom (x);
    denom := x ↑ 2 + sqrt (1 + 2 × x + 3 × x ↑ 2);
 alpha := (6.9 + y)/denom (y);
 beta := (2.1 × z + z ↑ 4)/denom (z);
 gamma := sin (y)/denom (y ↑ 2);
 delta := 1/denom (in (y))

The last example suggests that it would have been a good idea to call x by value; as it is, the sine will be computed three times in getting denom (sin (y)).

3. real procedure S34 (x, a);
    S34 := sqrt (x ↑ 2 − a ↑ 2);
 SFK := V × S34 (V, R)/2 − R ↑ 2/2 × ln (abs (V + S34 (V, R)));
 PSB := S34 (x [i], B) ↑ 7/7 + 2 × B ↑ 2 × S34 (x [i], B) ↑ 5/5
        + B ↑ 4 × S34 (x [i], B) ↑ 3/3;

There is no point to a call by value here, since each formal parameter appears only once in the procedure body. Nevertheless, both are inefficient, since the same function of the same parameters is computed several additional times. Much better:

 Temp := S34 (V, R);
 SFK := V × Temp/2 − R ↑ 2/2 × ln (abs (V + Temp));
 Temp := S34 (x [i], B);
 PSB := Temp ↑ 7/7 + 2 × B ↑ 2 × Temp ↑ 5/5 + B ↑ 4 × Temp ↑ 3/3;

5. real procedure Y (x);

$\qquad$ Y : = **if** x < 0 **then** 1 + sqrt (1 + x ↑ 2) **else if** x = 0

$\qquad\qquad$ **then** 0 **else** 1 − sqrt (1 + x ↑ 2);

F : = 2 + Y (a + z);

G : = (Y (x [k]) + Y (x [k + 1]))/2;

H : = Y (cos (6.28318 × x)) + 1 + Y (6.28318 × x);

7. real procedure sumnr (A, k);

$\qquad$ **begin real** sum; **integer** i;

$\qquad$ sum : = 0;

$\qquad$ **for** i : = 1 **step** 1 **until** k − 1, k + 1 **step** 1 **until** 20 **do**

$\qquad\qquad$ sum : = sum + abs (A [k, i]);

$\qquad$ sumnr : = sum

$\qquad$ **end**

It is very important not to use *sumnr* for accumulating the sum in the procedure body: doing so would require the procedure name to appear on the right-hand side of an assignment statement—which would be a recursive procedure body.

9. procedure Avernz (A, N, average, NZ);

$\qquad$ **begin integer** i;

$\qquad$ average : = 0;

$\qquad$ NZ : = 0;

$\qquad$ **for** i : = 1 **step** 1 **until** N **do**

$\qquad\qquad$ **begin**

$\qquad\qquad$ average : = average + A [i];

$\qquad\qquad$ **if** A [i] = 0 **then** NZ : = NZ + 1

$\qquad\qquad$ **end;**

$\qquad$ average : = average/N

$\qquad$ **end**

Avernz (Zeta, 20, Zmean, Nzcnt);

CHAPTER 8

1. format prob1 (4F8.0);

Read (prob1, BOS, EWR, PHL, DCA);

4. format prob4 (2I3, 2E14.7);

Read (prob4, LGA, IDL, BAL, ATL);

The "7" position in 2E14.7 is immaterial since the decimal point is punched.

5. format prob5 (I2, 10F7.0);

Read (prob5, N, **for** i : = 1 **step** 1 **until** N **do** data [i]);

7. The elements can be set up in any systematic order that is expressible in two nested for-statements. One simple way is to punch them in row order.

format prob7 (12I3);

Read (prob7, **for** i : = 1 **step** 1 **until** 3 **do**

$\qquad$ **for** j : = 1 **step** 1 **until** 4 **do** M [i, j]);

9. format prob9 (2F12.4, 2E20.8);

Print (prob9, A, B, X, Z);

11. format prob11a (PAGE, "MATRIX ABC");

format prob11b (4E20.8);

Print (prob11a);

Print (prob11b, **for** i : = 1 **step** 1 **until** 10 **do**

$\qquad$ **for** j : = 1 **step** 1 **until** 4 **do** ABC [i, j]);

INDEX

105